GW00585180

Same same, but different

Sally Wootton

PNEUMA SPRINGS PUBLISHING UK

First Published in 2011 by:
Pneuma Springs Publishing

Same same, but different
Copyright © 2011 Sally Wootton
ISBN: 978-1-907728-09-9

Editor: Bethan Seymour
Cover design: Billie Sharp www.innov8gd.com

World's most dangerous places 2006 – 2010, by Robert Young
Pelton. ComeBackAlive.com. Used by permission.

Rotary International www.rotary.org Group Study Exchange

Pneuma Springs Publishing
A Subsidiary of Pneuma Springs Ltd.
7 Groveherst Road, Dartford Kent, DA1 5JD.
E: admin@pneumasprings.co.uk
W: www.pneumasprings.co.uk

A catalogue record for this book is available from the British Library.

For dad, my inspiration for adventure

For mum, for always being proud of me

…and

For little Woo, who literally turned my dream into a reality

Acknowledgements

I am one of those people who actually read the acknowledgements section of a book just to see what personal touches the author has included and generally to be nosey. I now have my own personal thanks to make, because let's face it, it is quite exciting to actually get your words into print – even if the only people who buy your book are your mum and curious friends.

It quite literally started with my sister Tracy (Billie, little Woo), who after a few glasses of wine on a visit to stay with me, almost commanded that I write about my travels and who was the first person I trusted to tell that I was even writing a book. Tracy you are also my amazing designer and the professional with a personal interest. You designed a fantastic cover; painstakingly devoted your skills to turn my words into something people would be able to read and literally made my dream come true. I am more grateful for all your time and work than I can ever say—thank you.

Thanks to my first editor Beth, for being so brilliant and recognising all the mistakes, even when I was convinced they weren't there. Thank you to Pneuma Springs, for giving me the chance to realise my dream to publish my book. My best friend in the whole world, Sam – who rolled her eyes every time I mentioned I was even contemplating another trip, never read my emails from abroad and desperately, just hoped I'd someday settle down. But you have always supported me in everything I've done and I don't want to ever be without you (oh and I'll be testing you this time, so get reading). My friends James, Swede, Nick & Vicky, and Kirsty who were there when my travels started, Jo H (my friend most ridiculously excited about this book), Sam W (my most recent and now, regular travel buddy), Tash, Michele, Si, Rachel, Rowly, Paul and Talane and everyone who fuelled my excitement and encouraged me in the hope that anyone would be even vaguely interested in reading what I had to offer.

For Nanny Cole and Nanny Wootton, who I wish were both still here to read it and who's long sleeved vests kept me warm in Greenland. My many travel companions, Simon, Emma, Andy, Bobby, Steve, Anne and Kate and all the wonderful people I have met along the way, who've made my travels so colourful and for all those people, who after reading my emails said, 'You should write a book'.

Lastly, thank you to my mum and dad. Dad, if not for the times you encouraged me to push myself to do the things I was scared of and to try new things when I had the opportunity, I might never have developed the travelling bug. Mum, no matter what I wanted to do, you were always proud of me even when you couldn't understand why I wanted to do something. So this book is for you, my beloved parents. Thank you for being the best parents anyone could ever wish for. For believing in me in everything I've done, for supporting me when you didn't necessarily approve and for always being there at the arrivals gate, making coming home special too.

Same same, but different

And so it began

'Mum, can I go to Greenland?' I was just seventeen years old when I first got the travelling bug. I was at school, in the first year of my A-levels and had no real idea what I wanted to do with my life. I'd toyed with the idea of being a teacher when I was ten and liked to boss my sister around from the front of our pretend classroom and there was a time I thought I'd fancy being an architect, until I realised it required seven years of dedicated study. I'd never been further than the South of France on holiday with my parents and that was quite exotic considering the years of caravanning on the Isle of Wight and Cornwall.

Then one day as I sat, a newly appointed sixth former looking out onto the rest of the school and listening to another boring assembly, something caught my attention. The British Schools Exploring Society was running expeditions to remote locations of the world and inviting young people aged sixteen to twenty-three to join. It would be for seven weeks in the summer holidays, you raised the money yourself through sponsorship and hard work and got to travel and see the world.

I felt that little spark of excitement in the pit of my stomach, started imagining all the fantastic opportunities, already started planning how I could raise the cash and for the first time in my life I knew exactly what I wanted to do. I wanted to travel.

Since exploring Greenland back then, I've been lucky enough to travel all over the world and had some amazing experiences, met some wonderful people and survived more bad luck than should happen to one person. But, although I never forget how fortunate I am, I have made all of this happen myself. I have saved, planned, taken every available opportunity that came my way and had the courage to realise my dreams and in the process I have learned more about myself some good and some not so good – and my abilities.

7

This book isn't intended as a travel guide, or as a novel, but as a way of sharing my amazing experiences with others – those who have travelled and those who have yet to. But also to hopefully inspire those who've ever heard themselves say, 'I'd love to travel', but never thought they'd be able to, to realise that it is possible, if you really want it enough.

Greenland 1992

After months of saving, fundraising, collecting sponsorship and even selling my mum's rock cakes at school for extra cash, I embarked on what I still consider as seven of the most incredible weeks of my life.

I can remember saying goodbye to my parents; it was the first real goodbye of my life so far. The only other times I'd been away had been Brownie camp which didn't actually count – as my mum came as a helper – and the time she put me on a bus to Portsmouth to visit my pen friend and made the driver promise not to stop.

As I waved them off and went to join the rest of the group, I remember feeling incredibly independent, nervous, excited and hugely proud of myself. If I'm totally honest, I secretly still feel that way every time I go through departures at the beginning of any of my travels, even now and I'm thirty-six.

The group consisted of sixty young people to be divided into five groups of twelve, plus fifteen mountain and field leaders. We departed England and flew via Copenhagen to Narsarsuaq airport in South Greenland and had our first taste of what lay ahead.

Beneath us, as we came in to land while icicles formed on the plane windows, lay the most spectacular view of the ice cap. Miles and miles of untouched snow and ice, broken only by the occasional mountain peak, stretched as far as the eye could see. I looked out of the window of my first ever plane journey and felt totally overwhelmed at the prospect of what I was about to experience. It was a landscape I'd only ever seen on television or in books and I could hardly believe I was about to spend the next seven weeks of my life here.

Having never experienced any airport other than Heathrow, which we'd left fifteen hours previously, I realised that Heathrow it wasn't. The airport resembled something similar to a not particularly extravagant community hall and I don't think they'd ever seen so many people come from one flight. We excitedly collected our rucksacks and assembled for the one-mile trek to the overnight accommodation, an open-sided boat shed.

It was a wooden structure which had uprights, two ends, a floor and a roof, but what it lacked in home comforts, it more than made up for in location, as the scenery was breathtaking. Our shed stood on the banks of the fjord, surrounded by an imposing mountain range, with snow-capped peaks on the other side of the turquoise water. The colours weren't to be fully realised until the morning, but even in the glow of the moonlight, it was possible to appreciate the sheer scale of our surroundings and marvel at the glow from the snow in the darkness.

As we laid out our rucksacks and claimed a space on the wooden floor, I remember being too excited to sleep and listening to the quiet chatter of everyone else too full of anticipation to rest. I had already met my group and loved the fact that there were so many new and interesting people to get to know, from all over Britain, with so many different accents. In fact, that first night as everyone else drifted off to sleep, I had my first introduction to Viz magazine by torch light and a crash course in Geordie with the Newcastle contingent.

Eventually, overlooking the tranquil water of the fjord and with the only sound from a distant waterfall, we all drifted slowly off to sleep. We were woken in the early hours of dawn by a tremendous crash in the fjord. The noise – like a crack of thunder belonged to a large iceberg capsizing in the fjord literally only tens of metres from where we slept. It was amazing to see, yet strangely somehow like a warning – a reminder of the unpredictability and natural power of our new environment.

Now, in the bright sunshine of a new day, the sheer scale of the rugged mountains and ice-packed fjord and the beautiful purity of our surroundings were astounding. My only sorrow was that there would be no photograph or words able to portray its magnificence to people back home.

Civilisation... sort of

We left Narsarsuaq on a chartered fishing boat *The Taterak* for a twelve-hour voyage through fjords and open waters to the fishing village of Nanortalik. Now, when I say open waters, I'm not talking rolling oceans and I must point out at this stage that there was never a time when our view wasn't framed somewhere by a mountain range – it was merely their proximity that altered.

As we passed icebergs and watched the scenery around us, we heard the engines suddenly stop and the boat slowed. Before we knew it, the engines were back on but the boat was changing direction and seemed to be going off course. We soon discovered that the crew had sent a dinghy after a seal they had spotted and were now hunting it with harpoons. It was quite shocking at first, although we had to remind ourselves that this was their life and their livelihood and it became an interesting sight. I wasn't quite sure whether I was rooting for the crew or the seal after a while to be honest, but the seal lost and they dragged it on board to gut and clean, which I didn't watch.

I have to confess at this point that despite my passionate appreciation of the landscape, I was after all a teenager used to the comforts of home and it was, quite frankly, freezing. So, as we got tired of wiping our dripping and rather red noses, we went below deck to warm up.

We arrived in Nanortalik in the evening to be greeted by the advance party and countless curious locals. As we stepped off the boat and saw the crowds staring, grinning and advancing eagerly on us, I'm not ashamed to say I was momentarily a little disappointed. There seemed to be a distinct lack of authenticity compared to the fur-clad, textbook Eskimos I'd been expecting and these people were quite clearly dressed in jeans, parkers and trainers. While I realise that complaining about the lack of fur is somewhat controversial, in my defence I was very young and naïve. This is a culture that survives on local resources and I hadn't actually contemplated the possibility that they didn't live in little houses made of ice and wear head to toe fluff.

In reality, the Greenlanders are a combination of Danes and the native Inuit, scattered in picturesque settlements around the very fringes of the island. Due to the hostile landscape and conditions, farming is impossible and their only means of major trade, certainly back then, was fishing and hunting. During the summer, the hunting season thrives and stores are prepared for the winter months and needless to say, fishing is pretty much a constant.

We were shown to our temporary home, the local school, where we would stay for the next week while we waited for our supplies to catch up with us. As we went into the wooden schoolhouse, I looked around at the functional tables and simple furnishings and thought how ironically like my old Brownie hut it felt. Still, thankfully no one suggested playing blind man's bluff or singing campfire songs and we set about exploring the town.

Although Greenland's towns were as far from civilisation as we knew it, most of the larger settlements, among their modest-sized, colourfully painted wooden houses, boasted a school, hospital, post office, several small supermarkets, a bank, church, small hotel, town hall, at least one football pitch, a power station and of course, a fish and chip shop!

Another unavoidable feature of the town was the distinct and by no means pleasant odour of seal meat and dead fish. Outside many homes and shops, we saw lines full of small fish strung up to dry and slabs of gutted seal airing on rocks. Yet despite these obvious signs of primitive culture, there was the balance of modern-day living, as the mountain bikes and trucks used for transport demonstrated, along with the local nightclub for entertainment. Actually, I use the term 'nightclub' loosely, as it was more like a school disco and the drinking culture hadn't really evolved.

Our experience of Inuit drinking was that they would wait until payday, start on the local beer, which could be bought at something ridiculously expensive like £3 a bottle – in 1992, £3 for a bottle of beer was ridiculously expensive – and when their senses were sufficiently dulled, they'd switch to the local tipple, which wasn't entirely dissimilar to paint stripper. Needless to say, in a relatively small town, with very few tourists and a male-dominated population who drank a marginally more palatable version of meths, we didn't really go out in the evenings.

Generally though, the people were very friendly and our boys were challenged to several games of football, though I'm not sure any of us were certain of the correct rules. The Greenlanders' hospitality never faltered and it quickly became apparent that, although coarse and uncomplicated, they do enjoy a very good quality of life.

Base camp

We left Nanortalik with our new friends waving us off and began the six-hour boat journey to the smaller fishing town of Augpilagtok. We remained there for a further two days, exploring the local area, walking up the closer mountains and swimming in turquoise melt water pools.

With hindsight, I also realised by the end of the first week that given the distinct lack of laundry facilities, my great idea of taking only one week's worth of underwear wasn't so great! Plus, at the seemingly innovative suggestion of my mum at the time of packing, I had invested in the cotton equivalent of old lady's cycling shorts – as she said, "You'll need them for warmth, and they'll wash easily." I had also packed several of my Nan's thermal vests with sleeves, but had failed to pack any swimming gear, thinking wrongly that the last thing I'd ever be doing in sub-zero conditions was stripping off. So every time we swam, stripped off or had to hang our clothes out to dry, I would rather embarrassingly be the only one with underwear that had arms and legs.

We left Augpilagtok in shifts using two small inflatable motor boats to begin the final leg of our journey through almost solid pack ice, to base camp. Thanks to the expert manoeuvring of the boats by two Royal Marines, we dodged through the ice-packed fjord. Although there were times when we'd enter a break in the ice, only to find no way through ahead and the gap behind already closed.

We finally arrived at Prins Christian IV Island and the expedition proper began. We spent five hours working solidly, hauling all the supplies and equipment from the fjord, up the hazardous rocks and onto the lowland at the foot of the mountains. I don't think I'd ever worked so hard in my life until then and the stark reality that this was actually going to be quite tough began to dawn on me.

We pitched camp and experienced our first taste of living rough in the wilderness. As night quickly fell, the temperature dropped considerably, the rain began and tiredness gave way to a real low feeling that night. It was odd, so soon into the expedition, but I can only remember two other occasions when I felt as low spirited as I did that evening.

With the new morning though came blazing sunshine and higher spirits. Base camp was on very rough terrain, surrounded on two sides by the fjord, on another by the abandoned river valley cradling our study glacier and on the other by a towering mountainside. Throughout most of the expedition, the sun during the day was intensely hot, lasting until about 4.00 pm. Although daylight remained for a further six or seven hours, the temperature dropped rapidly and was often below zero by nightfall.

I had only ever camped before in our back garden with my sister or with the Brownies and Guides and we'd only ever used those great, heavy canvas tents, which acted like greenhouses in the heat. So even though these lightweight nylon versions were more modern and purpose-built, I spent the first few days trying to get used to the lack of space and unnecessarily trying not to touch the sides in case the rain leaked through.

I also very quickly noted the obvious lack of toilet facilities. No one had mentioned there wouldn't be any portable toilets and there most definitely wasn't a shower block, so it really was back to basics. To maintain some sense of dignity and civilisation, it was decided to have two separate toilet areas, one male and one female. These consisted of a man-made pit, away from our tents for obvious reasons and strategically situated behind a large rock. However, when I say man-made, I don't mean they were already there, previously trenched out by an obliging local for our convenience. We were the men and women making them and I have a rather unflattering picture of me waste deep in such a pit; shovel in hand, mid-dig. My second wake-up call.

So with the toilet facilities basic but adequate, the fjord as our washing-up water, a stream, our means of drinking supply and the glacier melt water as our bathing facility, there was really only one drawback of the low ground. The heat brought constant swarms of mosquitoes, continuously humming within inches of your face and feeding on any exposed flesh. Or non-exposed flesh too as it happened! Nothing would keep them away and for those of us who seem to give off an inexplicably inviting aura to the little beasts, there wasn't a patch of skin not swollen or itching.

Glaciology

Each group of twelve people, plus a leader, was allocated a study subject for the time we were to spend in the base camp and surrounding area and my group was to spend our time exploring the glacier.

After trekking for half an hour in the intense heat, carrying a load equal to about one-third of our body weight, I stepped for the first time onto the crystallised ice of a glacier. The ice was uneven and riddled with funnel holes and crevasses, treacherous ground to walk on without the correct equipment and great caution. The surface of the ice was also surprisingly dirty, littered with rocks and dust from the adjacent mountainsides. This was particularly apparent towards the edges of the glacier and caused, as we were soon to find out, by the rapid movement of the mass of ice, dislodging debris from the valley walls.

It was a strange experience to be able to look right down into the core of the glacier through the larger funnel holes into the ice. With depth, the ice becomes a darker blue, then black and the sound of running base water can be heard, even from the surface.

We spent three days at a mountain camp where we spent our time training for the dangers we might encounter out in the field. We learned how to prepare a snow camp to protect against storms, the safest way to haul ourselves out of a crevasse and how to rescue others using a belay system of ropes and harnesses. We were told what to do in a white-out, which is when a blizzard is so strong you can't determine where the snow you're standing on ends and the sky begins, and how to break a fall with an ice axe. But for me, the most daunting of all was learning how to ski.

Having only ever attempted dry slope skiing, I was horrified to discover, not only that I couldn't ski, but also that I could hardly even stand up. We would be skiing roughly five miles a day, cross-country once on the ice sheet, not only harnessed in groups of four, but carrying full loads as well. I started to dread the next few weeks and silently cursed how I'd previously underestimated the disadvantage of not being able to ski.

With the intense and succinct mountain training complete, we returned to base camp to begin our study work. Each day we travelled through the river valley and up the snout of the glacier, the easiest place to climb. We traversed the surface, determining the best survey site and then set up a base line and diamond-shaped formations of stakes to provide stations on which to focus our sightings from the valley sides.

We then carried the theodolite up the steep valley side and positioned the instrument to enable clear sighting of the stations and for easy communication via signals with the remaining group members on the glacier. Once we'd spent several days recording numerous readings to map the initial position of the glacier, we left the stakes in place for our return in three weeks. We would then repeat the process, obtaining results to enable us to measure the degree of movement of the valley glacier and determine its rate of retreat.

To gain more evidence of the glacier's recent retreat, we examined terminal and recessional moraine ridges. These are ridges of debris deposited by the glacier at its snout and secondary ridges caused by its retreat respectively. I happen to have had a particular interest in physical geography, as it was one of the lessons at school that I actually enjoyed and I also went on in the future to study a degree in land surveying.

However, as glamorous and technical as this all sounds, if I'm honest I have to admit that 'examining terminal and recessional moraine ridges' is actually an elaborate way of saying we spent monotonous hours accurately measuring the size of little pebbles, which unless you are a complete anorak, is actually mind numbingly boring.

On the whole though, having never encountered a glacier before and being a bit of a closet geography geek, I really enjoyed the time in the valley. It was generally quite interesting and if you're going to measure pebbles and dirt, where better to do it than surrounded by such fantastic scenery.

Our glacier was indeed absolutely awe-inspiring. However, it wasn't just the object of our study, but also the source of our water supply for bathing and washing. Subsequently, only those people that have ever experienced submersion in truly ice-cold water will be able to relate to the feeling of a thousand knives stabbing you all over and the shock of having your breath literally taken away as you swiftly go numb.

Those people who have been fortunate enough not to endure such an experience may be able to recall a time when too much ice cream or the downing of a slush puppy led to instant 'brain freeze'. Well, imagine that from your head to your toes, with nothing but an inadequately small towel to take away the sting and you'll understand why I only washed the bare minimum for ten days and my hair never saw shampoo until we returned to civilisation. This as it turns out, is apparently quite good for your hair once you get past the itchy, greasy stage.

Adventure

We were well established as a group by now, forging friendships and getting to know each other's strengths and weaknesses. Or put more honestly, discovering who you liked and clicked with and who annoyed you so much at times, you wanted to push them head first into the shit pit.

We did discover though that our ever-challenging circumstances and sometimes difficult experiences meant we had to learn quickly to put any differences aside and work effectively as a team.

The next stage for our group was the move along the fjord in ribs to our second glacier. However, the ice was beginning to enter the fjord at a rate of about four knots, making our intended destination beyond immediate reach and we settled for a temporary site some way up a steep mountainside, opposite a smaller carving glacier.

I'm aware that this sounds very incidental, but to do the difficulty of the journey to this camp any justice, I have to paint the whole picture. While we'd been dodging the pack ice along the increasingly narrow fjord, I was picturing our second camp as similar in terrain to the first and therefore relatively accessible. It had started to rain lightly and it was cold, but that's a given. We were surrounded on both sides and as far as we could see by steep imposing mountains, looming way into the sky. I had been marvelling at their stature while simultaneously thanking my lucky stars that we didn't have to climb them, when suddenly the boats started to approach the mountain base and the engines were cut.

I realised I had no lucky stars. We did have to climb them and we had to climb a long way. It was precariously steep, the rain made it slippery and it turns out, I hate climbing. By that I mean I hate climbing with no safety aid, carrying my body weight in gear that is dragging me backwards and being more than a little aware that there's every chance I could fall at any given point.

When we reached a safe place to camp and after a good night's rest, the climb proved more than worth it. Looking back, I think that location was one of the most beautiful of the whole region. Our camp, situated in a coarse, grassy clearing, overlooked the opposing mountains and ice-scattered fjord below. Enclosed by boulders leading to a false summit on two sides, we had our own secluded hideaway with our water supply from a churning melt water stream, cascading over the mountain's edge.

In the days that we lived on the mountain, we familiarised ourselves with the archaic military radio that was to be our only means of communication with base camp and the other groups. I'm not the most technical of people and soon worked out that operating the complicated array of buttons and switches and tuning into the right frequency was a job best left to the boys. Not only that, but the thing was huge and heavy and had to be lugged every evening to a suitably clear location to make the compulsory arranged transmission to report on our situation.

We also became quite accustomed to another familiar evening occurrence. Because of our remote northerly position and the clear, uncontaminated conditions, we often saw the green glow of the northern lights. I had only ever read about them before and had no idea what they would actually look like. In those early days, we would often see a glowing green streak appear in the sky late at night, which would somehow just materialise, not dissimilar to the Milky Way, just closer somehow. The stroke of colour never seemed to move, yet was always changing in shade and colour from green to yellow and turquoise and back again. It was stunning.

The initial climb had been so exhausting that the only time we ventured back down was to leave for good. We had to time our departure with a suitable opportunity to navigate the fjord ice and had to take our chance against the onset of our first Arctic storm. The rain was driving and the wind bitterly cold, the ground was saturated and the rocks dangerously slippery. If I had thought the climb up was difficult, the journey down was worse.

We had to pick our way cautiously and progress was slow, so when we eventually reached the fjord we were soaked through, freezing cold and weary. With the ice thickening fast, we had to wait for the Marines to arrive and had no choice but to sit tight and try to keep warm.

That evening sticks in my memory as one of the worst times of the expedition. It is these times of exhaustion, trying conditions and character-building experiences that are supposed to mould and shape us – I think if anybody had dared to tell me that at that point I'd have slapped them. Huddled under a communal bivvy sack, hardly speaking and with every muscle aching, I had never wanted to go home as much as I did then.

The Marines reached us and we made it to Swordfish Bay, further along the fjord, where they left us with low supplies and low spirits to pitch our third camp. I remember the following day clearly because it was one of the first lessons in tough luck I learned from my travels. We had walked up the valley towards the snowfield when the weather really broke. The heavens literally opened and the most torrential rain and gusting winds sent us fleeing back to camp to reinforce the tents and sit out the storm.

It was then that I found that my camera which had been in my pocket had filled with water, ruined the film (these were the days before digital) and all the pictures I'd taken already and wouldn't work anymore. I was totally devastated and couldn't believe I would have no way of recording the beauty of what I was seeing. But, there was absolutely nothing I could do and I had no choice but to hope I would be able to get copies of other people's pictures.

We had also been expecting to return to base camp after several days on the mountains and, having prepared as such, carried only minimum personal gear. The plan was for the Marines to attempt a journey through the ice to us, bringing with them travel equipment, extra essentials from our personal kits and supplies for the next two weeks. The ice was funnelling through the fjord at too fast a rate to even attempt a return journey with us all to base camp. But it also meant that we would see no one else for the next two weeks other than our mountain leader who would be joining us.

For four days we remained completely tent-bound seeing nothing but the inside of our shelter and two tent mates. Then, thankfully with a change in the weather, came the Marines.

The next two weeks held fantastic opportunities for our group. We had the run of the ice sheet, unmapped territory to explore and a whole playground of ice and snow to go wherever we chose.

There was, however, one problem. The radio was very bulky and heavy to carry and to take it up onto the ice sheet we would have to sacrifice two, maybe three days of food, meaning an earlier return. Nightly contact with base camp was imperative, yet our position once on the snowfield, surrounded by mountain ranges and the sheer distance, would surely make transmission impossible. We had to make a decision.

We had come this far and determined to make the most of the opportunity, the decision was unanimous. The radio would be left behind and food for seven days in the field split equally within the group. So with a message of explanation for the Marines, should they return again after our lack of contact, we left the bay and began the long and exhausting trek through the valley that would lead us to the ice sheet.

The valley climb took a whole day, so when we crossed the corrie – a steep-sided hollow at the head of the valley – it was early morning and the sun was bright. The sight that met our eyes when we touched on the snowfield was beyond belief. For miles around, there stretched a vast expanse of dazzling snow, broken only by the odd rock falls or displaced boulders from the mountains in the distance. It was like nothing I had ever seen before, so natural and so beautiful. To our right, at the bottom of the corrie lay a tarn, a small lake formed by a melted glacier, in absolutely stunning deep turquoise. It was here that we put on our skis and harnessed up for the part that I dreaded most, the ski across the ice.

The going was tough and very slow, with many of us still unsteady. I focused on the mountain in the distance that was to mark our camp that night and made a rough guess of about an hour's travelling time – my first mistake. When it comes to cross-country snow travel, you can ski for hours, passing no landmarks and never seem to be making progress. Distances are not always what they first appear to be.

More than five hours later we reached our destination. Fortunately for me, I had somehow managed to get a grip of the whole skiing thing in the last few hours and the technique had started to sink in. It's actually quite an effective way of travelling with heavy loads and two of the three groups we'd split into had made good progress. We dumped our kit and flaked out on the snow near the mountain base to wait for the last group.

In what turned out to be a very fortunate twist of fate, our mountain leader insisted that we move further away from the foot of the mountain and closer to some water-filled crevasses. So like sulky teenagers, we all reluctantly dragged ourselves up and moved position to pitch camp. That night as we slept, we were woken by a thundering, crashing noise from behind our camp that had everyone up and out of the tents in seconds. As we stood in the moonlight, we watched as an avalanche sent rocks and boulders crashing down the gully to land in the area we had originally chosen for our campsite. It was quite a stark reminder of our unpredictable and unmerciful environment and a few people stayed awake that night.

The next day was spent skiing and practising to gain confidence for the advance over the col (a pass between two mountain peaks). That day was a real achievement for me as we split into three groups, with the more skilled carrying heavier supplies and the less able on foot. I was placed in the middle group and as the least competent, I really had to push myself and we ultimately made great progress. We had to climb in skis up the snow hills leading to the col and that involved inching our way up sideways and leaning into the slope. When we had to traverse crevasses, we would have to find the narrowest and strongest point and ski over the deep gap using our skis as sort of bridges. It was amazing, if a little daunting at times, and when we pitched camp that night I felt so proud.

We stayed only long enough to rest and then return the following morning to our previous camp briefly before moving on to the unmapped ice sheet. Three of us were nominated that morning to collect the belongings left behind and I was one of them. So, with my newfound confidence and the encouragement of one of my team members, we childishly started to race each other down the glacier following our mountain leader. Needless to say it was always going to end in tears, which were mine as it turned out. My ski hit the wall of the track we'd made the day before and in what I like to remember as a spectacular stack, I did a perfect cartwheel and landed ski first in the snow, wrenching my left knee in a direction it's not meant to go.

Still, not one to let a minor injury put me off and scared stiff I'd be sent home if I admitted how much it hurt, I struggled to my feet, confident nothing was broken and played it down. We made the rest of the journey, though somewhat more sedately, and I kept a low profile, trying to rest my leg whenever I could. I still to this day have no idea what I did to my leg in that fall, but the next morning the pain was incredible and I couldn't move my leg without it screaming at me.

I just remember feeling so worried that I'd be shipped back to base camp somehow and miss such a fantastic opportunity that I was determined not to waste the precious time left. I spent the next day walking with the slower group to the rognon (outcrop of rock), while the others skied and planned the trip for the next day. The plan was to ski from our camp to the rognon; deposit overnight supplies and then continue to the east coast before retracing our steps to the rock and sleeping under the stars.

The journey would take us through spectacular scenery, crossing uncharted territory to the fjord beyond, onto the east of the ice sheet and would be impossible for the slower members of the group to complete.

The sensible option would have been for me not to have attempted such a challenge on my injured leg, but I wasn't about to miss out and so insisted I was more than capable. Consequently, I still suffer now with the throbbing pain in my knee.

We started at 8.30 am the following morning, the snow was still crisp and everyone was full of determined anticipation. The first stage was straightforward and skiing was uneventful, if a little uneasy for some. We roped up to traverse the crevasse field and then made our way slowly uphill to the rognon where we deposited supplies for the following day and continued on the long ski across the ice sheet. I was surprised at how little my knee hurt when I was moving and I managed to hold my own and keep up with the rest of the group and it was worth it.

After a day of skiing on flat and seemingly endless snow, we reached our goal – the east coast. The view was spectacular. A huge carving glacier riddled with crevasses swept down towards the fjord below, ending in a deathly drop. The mountain ranges forming the sides of the fjord were incredible in their scale and beauty, while the fjord itself was an electric blue littered with pure white floating icebergs. A true winter wonderland.

I could have stayed there absorbing that scene forever. But the wind was bitingly cold and our body temperatures soon dropped once we stopped for long. We had no choice but to keep going, but that memory will stay with me as one of the most beautiful places I have ever been.

The return journey was long but we kept a steady pace. I remember being extremely tired and no one spoke, but we all felt an amazing sense of achievement. I know that I felt I could do absolutely anything having pushed myself that day. Sheer enthusiasm and determination kept me going and I felt so much stronger.

The following day was our last on the ice sheet and we spent our time clearing up and preparing for the ski back to the valley camp, which we'd decided to do in one journey. We were all quite subdued on that last day, sad to be leaving our playground and feeling physically drained.

As we settled down, it was a remarkably clear night without a single cloud or star to be seen and then we saw the familiar green glow. The northern lights stretched across the sky in a stroke of wispy green. The streak, in constant motion, changed in shape and shade until the entire sky seemed filled with the bright green glow. Gradually, the sky began to swirl like some ethereal vortex. The light moved in a large circular motion indeterminably changing from green to yellow then green again, until suddenly the swirling burst into amazing colour and the whole sky actually looked alive.

I have never seen anything so incredible in all my life and wouldn't have believed, or appreciated, it if someone else had tried to describe it to me. The entire sky was just dancing in an ever-changing swirl of colours, like a floating kaleidoscope. I often look back on that night and still marvel that I was privileged enough to witness such a rare and extraordinary display.

The following morning we were on our way back to base camp. Having pretty much mastered the skiing now we traversed the snowfield, bypassing our previous two camps and reaching the tarn in five hours. The sun was blazing hot by now and the tarn marked the end of the snowfield and the start of the tundra valley walk to the fjord. We sat drinking water and stripping off layers of clothing while we waited to regroup. It was bizarre how hot it was when you were surrounded by ice and snow and I looked up to see the Geordie appear round the side of the rock with his skis slung over his shoulders and wearing just a pair of red shorts and his sunglasses.

The three-hour trek down the valley proved our exhaustion, as our legs constantly gave way under our weight and we stumbled and staggered on loose rocks. Twenty-four hours later we were back at base camp. Our explanation about the radio wasn't well received, but we all agreed that faced with the same situation again, we'd have made the same decision.

As we exchanged stories and experiences with the other groups, we felt overwhelmed with relief. The past six weeks had been amazing, with wonderful memories, remarkable achievements and great new friendships. But I was physically and mentally exhausted and ready to go home.

We returned to the glacier to conclude our study, but found it had moved to such an extent that those stakes, which had not disappeared under the bulk of the ice, were now strewn on the surface, making any further research impossible. We had grown familiar to the formation of the glacier's snout in the initial period spent at base camp and now, just some three weeks later even at a glance, its alteration was obvious.

After closing down base camp and returning to Nanortalik for a few days of eating normal food, sleeping and feeling very emotional, we boarded our ferry to the airport in Narsarsuaq. I think that at this point the excitement of knowing we were on our way home gave way to the sadness of knowing one of the most incredible experiences of our lives was coming to an end.

It wasn't until we were all settled on the plane and the engines started with a huge thrust that I appreciated how very short the runway was. I have never, in all my years of flying, experienced such a short, sharp, loud and powerful take-off. We literally seemed to climb over the mountains, instead of making height before we reached them. As the mountains dropped away beneath us, we had our last view of the ice cap, no longer a strange new land, but a cherished part of our lives.

So, that was my first real experience of travelling and it more than whetted my appetite. I admit, it was a once-in-a-lifetime kind of trip and a hell of a way to start, but it certainly made me realise that there is a whole world out there and with a little bit of effort and determination, it isn't beyond reach.

I came back from Greenland and threw myself into my A-levels and then went on to university, where I hardly had the means to support my socialising never mind travelling. I did the usual sun holidays to Greece, which I loved and Turkey – which I didn't – and at twenty-one had a family holiday to the States where I stood with all the other kids to meet Mickey Mouse. Then when I finally graduated I considered working abroad, but eventually opted to start work and save for the next trip and the next and the next.

Canada 2000

If I haven't been to a country for more than a few weeks or really travelled around it then I don't consider that to be a real travelling experience, it's just a holiday or a quick stopover. The trouble with that mentality of course is that I either have to travel on a shoestring, or tend to spend a shorter space of time packing as much into a trip as possible and basically come home knackered.

I have no idea where my interest in visiting Canada came from, but even when I was at university I had a real desire to go there and see the Rocky Mountains and Niagara Falls. The main problem with that is that they happen to be on opposite sides of a very large country.

Still, not one to let a detail like geography get in the way, I set about researching all the places I wanted to go, the things I wanted to see and do and how I would travel between them. When I started looking at Canada and realised how vast and mountainous it actually is, I decided there was probably only two ways to really see the Rockies – by horseback or Winnebago. Actually they weren't really Winnebagos, but that sounds much better than the geeky-sounding 'recreational vehicle' (or RV to the real anoraks).

Anyway, I'm not overly keen on horses and they'd have struggled with my suitcase so we opted for an RV for the West coast from Calgary to Vancouver Island and then decided to fly to the East and do the cities in a hire car. I travelled with my boyfriend at the time and thankfully we proved to be one of those couples that could spend a month in the confines of a vehicle for twenty-four hours a day, without wanting to kill each other.

In fact, we happened to get lucky and the said vehicle was upgraded with no extra charge to a twenty-four foot, brand new version of the RV we had booked, so when we went to pick it up it was like a hotel on wheels. We couldn't believe our luck and quickly drove away in case the rental firm realised they'd made a mistake.

For two people, I have to say that particular RV was nothing but extravagant and we could have comfortably accommodated a family of four. There were two double beds over six feet in length, with one curtained off at the back forming a separate bedroom. We had a full shower room and separate toilet, family-sized fridge, dining table for four with an additional swivel armchair, oven, microwave and more storage space than we could even try to fill.

The Rockies

We started our trip in Calgary with a quick visit to the Calgary Olympic Park and saw the facilities from the winter events in 1988, including the bobsleigh run. When I say quick visit, I don't mean that we didn't stay for long, I mean that we took the 1,500-metre bobsleigh run at eighty-five kilometres per hour, in seventy-five seconds.

From Calgary, we started our journey towards the Rocky Mountains and I have to say I was so excited I was like a grinning child. A friendly Canadian at the airport had given us a cassette tape (honestly, cassettes were still around then) which instructed us to press play at a certain point along the route and gave a running commentary on the landmarks and approach to the mountains.

I remember, as we got closer, that the narrator informed us we would be seeing what looked like low cloud on the horizon right about now and that it would appear quite dark as we approached. He then proceeded to explain that this 'cloud' was actually the shadow of the mountains looming in the distance and that we now had our first sighting of the Rockies.

I was all 'Wow!' and gasps and totally enthused and as we drove closer and closer it felt like we weren't just seeing stunning mountains, but a famous landmark we were totally overawed by.

As we crossed the border entering the National Park, it was impressively clean and well maintained and everything was so naturally preserved. Any man-made additions, whether road signs or buildings or even just fencing, were ruggedly blended into the surroundings as best they could be and the sheer scale of the place was astounding.

The camping grounds and car parks all over Canada are designed with generous parking for RVs and the national camp sites have hook-up facilities for water, drainage and electricity and are so amazingly clean you could comfortably live in them on a permanent basis – quite a bit different to any camping experience in the UK.

Having said that, the weather wasn't much different at some points and we awoke the following morning to heavy rain. Nevertheless, heavy rain doesn't matter quite so much when the views all around are of snow-capped peaks and you can go from the breakfast table to the driving seat in your pyjamas if you want to. We didn't though, that would have been really embarrassing if we'd been stopped.

We went for a walk around Banff and even in the rain it was like a beautiful Alpine village. All the shops were really picturesque with little fairy lights and the impressive Gothic-inspired Banff Springs Hotel looks down from its grand mountainside position. I think Banff was one of the prettiest towns I remember from Canada, although there's something a little too perfect about it. It's almost as if it has been modelled directly on something out one of those snowstorms you have as a child, where you shake them and the snowflakes float to the bottom of the dome.

We then drove up the mountain where we had to stop to let several Elk pass and couldn't resist getting out for a quick photo opportunity. We took the gondola ride to the top of the mountain and had a coffee overlooking the town. You could feel the difference in the air quality and, if only there had been no cloud cover, we would have been able to see for miles.

Towards the end of the day we drove to Lake Minnewanka (honestly) to see if we could spot a grizzly bear. Foolish really, seeing as half the park was closed off to the public due to the six bears on the prowl, which had already charged several vehicles and a cyclist that day. Still, bears charging vehicles and breaking into picnic boxes was one of those things you only ever hear about on television, it never actually happens to anyone you know. As we sat with our cup of tea at the deserted lakeside, the reality of the regular radio bulletins and the fact we had been given a verbal and written warning as we entered the area, started to sink in and we decided to leave after all, just in case.

We left Banff the following day to travel to Lake Louise, but not before taking a long, luxurious and very smelly dip in the mineral hot springs at the foot of Sulphur Mountain. You'd think the name would have given it away, but the smell was foul. The outside pool was like sitting in a hot bath with steam all around you, the views were amazing and we were in the Rockies, but the smell of rotten eggs took the edge right off.

When I saw Lake Louise for the first time, I couldn't believe the colour. It was like the turquoise of the lakes in Greenland, but a deeper green and cloudy from the quartz bed. The lake sits in a valley surrounded by the mountains and huge carving glaciers, which eventually merge into one at the mouth of the valley.

I remember someone once telling me that Lake Louise was not really worth visiting because it was just all trees and the lake and the only other thing there was the chateau. I think he must have had his eyes shut the whole time because it's the most beautifully peaceful and serene place. True, it's not exciting and crazy and once you've taken a canoe across the lake, walked the four-hour round trip to the glacier and dreamed of being able to stay in the £200 per night chateau, you've pretty much exhausted it, but it's definitely not to be missed.

We moved on to the Ice Fields Parkway next and it was my turn to drive the RV. Probably not the best initiation to driving a twenty-four foot vehicle, with the route being through relatively narrow and climbing mountainsides, but more worryingly the scenery was stunning and I'm notoriously easily distracted.

I don't have to describe how excited I was to be going up onto the glacier – I think the Greenland chapter pretty much covers that. We took a snow truck up the Athabasca Glacier and although it was sunny on the low ground, it seemed to be driving a mini blizzard on the surface and I confess I was as keen as everyone else to get back to a nice hot chocolate.

We stayed the night in Jasper, which isn't as pretty as Banff, but distinctly more rugged and cowboy-like. In fact, the following morning, we threw ourselves into the mountain way and went horseback riding. Now, as I've said before, horses aren't my favourite animals and my only previous experience was on a psycho pony at Butlins when I was eleven and it pretty much put me off from then on.

But, when in Rome and all that, so we saddled up and a group of about ten of us set off through the forest. The ranch owner had two funny, little rat-like terrier dogs that ran out upfront, supposedly to detect bears and warn them off. They were quite fun to watch and dodged in and out of the horses hooves, before darting off for several minutes and then running back again yapping. Apart from their entertainment value though, I couldn't quite work out how they would be any form of deterrent to bears. I imagine it would be similar to King Kong being driven out of town by an overexcited hamster and can only shudder at their inevitable fate if we had happened upon a grizzly.

I'd like to say that I had a pleasant experience on the horse and revaluated my opinion of them, but suffice it to say, my horse had a mind of its own. It appeared that I had the only horse with an aversion to getting its feet wet. So whenever we came to a puddle or particularly boggy area of mud, it would seek out the driest alternative – and usually precarious – route and head for it, which was mildly unnerving and I was glad to get down after an hour.

The landscape is so beautiful and rugged through the Rockies that we spent several days just walking through the forests, visiting waterfalls and enjoying the last of the scenery before we had to head out of the National Park and hit the highway heading west.

Beyond the mountains

As soon as you leave the park area, it is immediately obvious with all the billboard signs and flashing neon, indicating hotels and diners at the sides of the road.

We travelled through Clearwater to Harrison Hot Springs, a small town notorious locally for its mineral pools and as we discovered, annual sandcastle competition. I realise that on the face of it that doesn't sound too impressive and I wasn't particularly interested either, until we realised they weren't just ordinary sandcastles, they were actual works of art. The sand is apparently shipped in especially for the event and people from all over the world gather for the three-day event. The finished products stand over ten feet high and take all forms – from sculptures of the Taj Mahal, Queen Boudicca in her chariot to the man in the moon.

Despite the impressive efforts of the various entries, it rained heavily while we were there and we didn't have the heart to wait to see if they were all still standing for judgement day.

Our next stop was Vancouver Island and we managed to squeeze our motor home on to the alarmingly small ferry, whose seats I am certain were donated from the local old people's homes. We drove straight to Tofino and booked our whale-watching trip for the following day. From August through December, the orcas, or killer whales, migrate southwards to breed in Mexico and we had planned to go out on a partially glass-bottomed boat to see if we would be lucky enough to spot any.

When we boarded the boat, it was surprisingly small and the glass bottom turned out to be a panel about a metre in length at the back of the boat. There was seating on wooden benches for about eight at the rear, a cab for the captain and seating for two at the front, where we sat and had the most exhilarating ride, bouncing off the waves and getting thoroughly soaked. When the captain cut the engines, we looked around at each other and had no idea what we were supposed to be seeing.

The captain, though, knew exactly what he was doing and he pointed out to sea where we saw the distant breaking of the water by the lumpy back of a grey whale. It was amazing and although the greys were in the distance and too far for us to get good pictures, we saw about four or five of them breaching. It was quite surreal to think we were floating in the same water as these huge great creatures were swimming, only a short distance away.

We kept our eyes peeled and eagerly watched the surface of the sea, looking for the next sighting. Then the captain began to shout. He was a really experienced sea man and had many years of taking tourists out to view the whale migrations, but there he was jumping around and pointing frantically into the water, not too far from where we were. When we all looked in the same direction, we saw three orcas breaching and their tails forming the familiar sight we had all seen on television or in books. We kept scanning the surface, waiting to see them again, but not quite knowing where to direct our attention, until suddenly there a whale was just metres from the boat.

I have no idea how something so huge came so close to our boat, without turning it over, but if we had reached out far enough we could have touched it. It was so sleek and graceful and seemed to be checking us out before it passed right underneath us, causing little more than a slight ripple.

Our next few days were spent relaxing and catching up with a friend in Vancouver before we went to brave the Capilano suspension bridge. I had never been on a suspension bridge before, so although a friend of mine has since assured me that Vancouver's version is mild compared to the hair-raising feats of engineering in Costa Rica, I was quite apprehensive. It sits 230 feet above the ground and spans 450 feet of forest and much to my naive horror, they let more than one or two people cross it at a time. That wouldn't have been so bad, but you always get someone who thinks it's funny to try and scare everyone and as it's essentially just a rope bridge tied to some planks of wood, it shakes very easily.

Our next stop in Vancouver was through the very Londonesque Stanley Park to the shopping centre and beyond. I say beyond because after a brief wander around the city centre we happened to find ourselves in some very dark-looking streets, with some very dark-looking people and realised we'd happened upon downtown. You don't like to judge, just because there are gangs of people on street corners with tattoos, ripped clothing and chains linking their noses to their ears. But when we passed someone screaming madly and bashing his own head and saw the rather intimidating way we were being eyed up as we passed, we held our bags firm and swiftly headed back in the direction we'd come from.

Fortunately, we headed in a more appealing direction and ended up at the marina where we were surrounded by luxurious boats and yachts, giving the impression of a Cannes-style setting. After climbing aboard a few of those for sale, I picked out a rather impressive three-storey cruiser, with double en-suite bedrooms, a party deck and a little too much cream leather and was just trying to imagine myself sipping champagne at the helm, when I saw the price tag! Admittedly, it was never a realistic daydream anyway, but when they offer marine mortgages, you realise you're not Madonna and have less than no chance of draping yourself over the cream leather of your own yacht.

The East Coast

So, back to reality as we said goodbye to the west coast and flew the six hours across country to the east. We decided to hire a car on the east side and stay in hotels, with our first stop being the small city of Quebec in the French province. Quebec is beautiful and the city equivalent of Banff in the Rockies. The road signs are all in French and that is the first language of the people there, whom we had been warned, were quite reluctant to speak English.

In fact, you almost feel more awkward about not being able to speak French in Canada than you do when you visit France. It's oddly like stepping into a parallel universe, in a vast country where everyone speaks English, to this relatively small sector, where everyone is from an entirely different culture, with a different language and different rules. Sort of like Cornwall, but more cosmopolitan!

Without a prior booking, we found ourselves struggling to find a bed for the night and had to settle for a rather basic, unappealing little lodging – which at $45 for the room probably speaks for itself. We had a lovely meal in a typically French restaurant, where for the first time I tasted 'lapin' (rabbit, it tastes like chicken) and then ventured back to our hovel, where after a hectic day we slept very well – once we had picked the hairs out of the bed.

Quebec was very picturesque, even in the very cold and wet weather. We spent our time very decadently wandering from café, to church, to creperie and admiring all the quaint shops and art galleries. Our meal that evening was possibly the best meal I have ever had in a restaurant, even to this day. We found the most beautiful little French restaurant with a romantic courtyard, lit by white fairy lights and exotic plants.

When our meals arrived, I have to admit that at first, my thoughts were 'Is that all?' and resolved to find a pizza hut on the way home. But the food was so rich and so perfectly balanced that after my 'cappuccino' lobster bisque, caribou steak with mini poached vegetables and all-time favourite crème brûlée, I was perfectly full.

We ended our time in Quebec with a rather sophisticated visit to a very chilled out little jazz bar. It was one of those truly cool places, where we sipped cocktails while listening to the piano and saxophone, perched on bar stools that were too high to be at all comfortable for short people and felt quite frankly, if I'm honest, right out of my league.

That feeling wasn't helped at all by my insistence on ordering a vodka martini, just because after watching too many James Bond films, I'd always wondered what one tasted like. It turns out, not altogether surprisingly, that they taste exactly like vodka mixed with martini, which is in fact extremely strong. For someone whose tipple of choice had always been a pint of cider and black, or whichever watered down promotional cocktail happened to be on offer at the time, the sudden introduction to an actual cocktail complete with undiluted alcohol and decorative olive was a somewhat rude awakening.

The next city was Montreal, which as Canada's second largest city, is much bigger than Quebec, still in the French Province and divided into Quarters. One of the most notable features of Montreal is its architecture. The city successfully manages to merge the old with the new and still retain its seductive sense of culture and history. There are some amazing buildings such as the Basilique Notre-Dame and plenty of old warehouses and houses converted into restaurants, shops and condos and then the new, sleek modern structures which somehow seem to blend right in. The Saint Lawrence River flows through the city and its banks provide the stage for street performers and shows, while the Latin Quarter boasts plenty of Bohemian street cafes and restaurants.

We visited the beautiful Botanic Gardens and the Olympic Park, where we walked through a stunning night-time Chinese garden lit up by hundreds of tiny lanterns with beautiful exotic flowers. The city also has a complex underground metro system and I think it's fair to say that after several hours trawling the shops and buying relatively little by my standards, we'd probably covered most of its tracks.

We didn't have too much trouble with the language in Montreal for people that speak almost no French. As usual, its reputation wasn't quite in line with the reality and most people were only too happy to take over in English once we'd attempted the obligatory Del Boy-style 'bonjour' and a rather lame attempt at beginning to ask for whatever we required.

Moose and waterfalls

Toronto was our next and penultimate destination and probably my least favourite city on the east coast. I wouldn't say there was anything particularly to dislike about Toronto, but for me unless a city has something extraordinary, then I feel you can have similar experiences in many western cities alike.

There were, however, two rather unique attractions for me in Toronto – the CN tower and moose! The CN tower, once the world's tallest man-made structure, stands at approximately 550 metres high and has views as far as Niagara Falls. It also overlooks Lake Ontario, which hosts its own airport and is so big you can't actually see the other side from the top of the tower. The scale is pretty clear, yet I still found myself worrying about the fact I had a skirt on while walking across the glass floor of the viewing deck!

As for the moose, well they were a pretty unusual and unfortunately temporary attraction. The city was to our great amusement hosting an exclusive art exhibition across the centre, which consisted of 375, eight-foot high, moulded moose randomly placed on street corners, park fountains, building overhangs and other public places and dressed in various different themes. There were among the many inventive styles, a bridal moose, soldier moose, ABBA moose, a Mountie moose and even an Elvis! My only regret was not having taken more pictures, but as I previously pointed out those were the days before digital technology.

Probably one of the most anticipated highlights of Canada for me was Niagara Falls. It was certainly the main reason I had orchestrated the trip to include the east coast as well as the west and I had all sorts of images in my mind of what it would be like. Unfortunately and, perhaps naively, I hadn't anticipated the over commercialised, water's edge skyscraper hotels and restaurant complexes, which mar the natural wonder of the landscape.

That's not to say the man-made eyesores completely ruin the impression or sheer magnificence of the falls, but undoubtedly their absence would make for a far more unspoiled experience.

Having satisfactorily aired my opinion about the disappointing and glaring impact of tourism, I promptly joined the queue for the Maid of the Mist tourist attraction, along with about fifty other promotional

'Maid of the Mist' poncho-clad holidaymakers and eagerly waited in line for our boat trip to the base of the falls.

While we waited for our boat, I looked on curiously as a couple of over enthusiastic Japanese women produced cagoules, shower caps, surgical booties and all manner of other types of wearable clear plastic and gradually covered every inch of their clothed bodies. I then watched with growing amusement as they took picture after picture of each other and seemed oblivious to the stares of everyone shaking their heads at how ridiculous they looked.

Ridiculous that was until we approached the base of the torrential cascade of water, which proceeded to saturate each and every one of us as we scrambled to find cover – all of us that is, apart from two smugly dry Japanese women.

Nevertheless, the scale of the cascading water and the thunderous noise was mesmerising and absolutely spectacular. It is possible to ignore the hundreds of other people gathering to stare from both the Canadian and USA border points, which flank the falls, and to block out the buildings around you and just get lost in the wonder of Niagara Falls. It is exactly like all the pictures you see and is in itself an absolutely amazing natural phenomenon.

I would like to end my depiction there, but unfortunately I can't sincerely conclude without reluctantly describing the horror of Niagara by night. For all the beauty and natural wonder of Niagara by day, the Canadians have technologically vandalised the falls by inflicting a tacky light display of changing stripes of colour across its arc, comparable only in its tackiness to the Blackpool illuminations.

So Niagara brought my dream to a close. I had explored Canada, the place I had wanted to travel my whole adult life and it had lived up to all my expectations. However, I still felt the need to have my own adventure, alone. I wanted to travel on my own, with no one else to answer to and no one else to consider and to just do my own thing.

I have always enjoyed my own company and as all my friends know, I like to have my solitary time where I can just be as free from obligation as I want to be. I realised that I needed to do a trip for me and having lived my adult dream, the obvious destination seemed to be my childhood dream, Australia.

Australia 2003 – down under

As an impressionable ten-year-old, big into watching *Neighbours* and a paid-up member of the Kylie Minogue fan club, I developed the predictable dream of someday going to Australia. In fact, I can still remember defiantly declaring to my mum as I watched her cook that I would one day visit Australia. Lest she doubt my sincerity, I emphasised that my trip would be for at least two weeks and promptly started planning – until dinnertime!

Although I felt the need to travel alone as I planned my trip to Australia, the reality of doing so seemed far more daunting than the dream and circumstances provided the opportunity for me to travel with a friend from my university days.

True to form, I carefully researched and organised my trip according to the places I really wanted to visit and the things I particularly wanted to see while there. The *Rough Guide* had become my bible while in Canada and soon proved as useful in Australia. I would always advocate to anyone who is planning to travel, to read a few travel guides, research on the internet before you set off and have a rough idea of the things you feel you must see and do, but also to allow for flexibility along the way.

If you have no plan then you will inevitably drift and miss out on amazing places you would have loved to go, had you known about them. If you plan too meticulously and aren't impulsive every so often, then you will inevitably miss out on amazing opportunities you would have loved to experience, had you let them happen.

For me, every journey I take begins at the airport. This might seem obvious, but I don't mean in the physical sense. I mean that every time I step foot in an airport, the excited little child inside me wakes up and I feel like I'm on holiday for the first time ever. Actually, if I'm honest that starts as soon as I shut my front door and get into the car to travel to the airport, as anyone who's ever had the misfortune of travelling with me will know.

I can't help it, I even feel that way when I take domestic flights in this country. There's just something about getting rid of your bulky bags at check-in and having the sense of having nothing else to do but relax and shop, drink, eat, sleep, read or do whatever you want until you start your journey. It could even possibly be just the fact that you are having a break from your reality, whatever that is day to day.

But whatever the reason, for me it's still that magical feeling I used to get when I was a little girl, going on holiday and travelling in the middle of the night so the roads were quiet. When your body was all weary from not being able to sleep for excitement, but so overtired, your eyes ached because you didn't want to miss anything. I still get that feeling whenever I travel, even now. The difference is, these days I can stop to go to the loo whenever I want, without my dad grumbling at me and I have the ability to sleep like a log, excited or not.

Australia is about a twenty-one hour flight, with a stop to refuel. So that means twenty-one hours of sitting down, chilling out and reading, watching cool films, drinking free alcohol and being fed every few hours, in between flexing your ankles and avoiding DVT. I also love plane journeys, the longer the better. But then I have short legs.

I met my friend Andy and some of his friends at Sydney airport and they took me to Bondi where one of them had an apartment for the summer. I could hardly believe it – from the moment we arrived it was gloriously sunny, we were actually in Bondi and I was, as ever, totally uncool with excitement. There is only one thing to do in Bondi, which is to hit the beach. Well actually the one thing to do in Bondi is surf, but I don't surf. I do, however, swim and I do drink beer, lots of beer, so who needs surf?

Approximately four hours after landing and one 'schooner' of beer later – a schooner is the Aussie equivalent of just over half a pint – I was dead on my feet and feeling the lethargic effects of jet lag. Bondi nightlife would have to wait and the only thing I was fit for was sleep.

A familiar bridge ...

As it turned out, sleeping was all I was fit for for several days until the jet lag wore off. We spent the days exploring Sydney and the area around Bondi and for some reason I found myself amusingly surprised at the sight of the Opera House and Harbour Bridge. Having seen them plenty of times in pictures and on television, I knew exactly what to expect, but actually seeing them for the first time it was almost as if I felt surprised they were real.

In fact, I had an odd sense that I had seen the Harbour Bridge somewhere before, but having never been to Sydney before, it took a few minutes before I remembered it was modelled on the Tyne Bridge. So having lived in Newcastle for eight years, I had effectively spent a considerable amount of time looking at it before I ever actually saw it.

The view across the harbour from the bridge is fabulous and probably one of the most familiar sights associated with Australia. Less familiar, however, is the view from the summit point of the steel arch of the bridge, 440 feet above sea level and having done the organised bridge climb, was somewhere I discovered that I can take or leave heights.

I also discovered that the Australians are generically fitness crazy. While we lounged around Bondi and neighbouring Coogi, the most energetic thing we did was take a slow walk along the stunning coastal path, interspersed with breaks at any available bar or café, drinking anything cold and wet and keeping out of direct sunshine.

The Australians, however, took any opportunity to walk, jog or run along the same coastline and appeared to not even notice that it was forty-five degrees. I remember training for the north run in a freakishly hot English summer one year and having badly timed a session, I nearly passed out from a gentle jog at midday. Yet the Aussies seem to let nothing stand in their way of achieving ultimate fitness and train at any time, in any temperature. That said, I don't think I saw one fat Aussie and there's a lot to be said for a penchant for working out, when they spend the majority of time in board shorts and bikinis.

Before we left Sydney for the first leg of our journey along the south coast, we celebrated Australia Day. Australia Day is a national holiday, on 26 January and is solely for the purpose of celebrating with national pride, what the Aussies love about their country. A day to 'celebrate what's great' is the motto. To everyone therefore, Australian or not, it is either a family holiday or a day off work to get totally and utterly trollied.

We did the latter and celebrated 'what's great' all day long. In fact, I seem to recall among my last memories of that night, mischievously joining forces with my English friend Emma and taking great joy in winding up the locals of one rather dodgy-looking pub. Fuelled by a little too much amber nectar, we'd point at the Union Jack on the Aussie flag, while bellowing 'Rule Britannia' and claiming that was the 'great' thing about Australia. Not one of my proudest moments I admit, but then not one of my most sober either and it was nonetheless very amusing at the time – until we got thrown out.

The outback and the huntsman

The best way to travel around Australia if you haven't got a car is by bus. Not keen to be on a party bus full of newly graduated students, intent on blasting their way round Oz in a drunken stupor, I opted for the more independent Greyhound for most of the road trip. Not that I want to paint a distorted picture of my own sobriety, which would be a tad hypocritical and readily refuted by anyone who knows better. But I did at least want to make the most of every day of my trip and there was too much to be done to waste any of it.

Some of my time was spent using the buses as a means of getting from A to B and then booking my own accommodation as I pleased. But for the south coast leg of the journey, I opted for an organised tour bus, where you stay with the same group of people for a number of scheduled days and everyone stays in the same pre-booked accommodation. It is slightly more restrictive, but a great way to meet new people and build up confidence to travel alone.

The schedule from Sydney to Adelaide along the south coast takes just six days, twelve hours of driving every day, which means getting up very early. We left Sydney and drove through Canberra for a fleeting visit of the capital city. I was surprised at how clinical and soulless it seemed, but then we only visited the embassy buildings and war memorials and didn't actually spend much time there at all.

From what I could gather, the main reason they decided to make Canberra the capital city was because they couldn't decide between Sydney or Melbourne so decided it would be neither and picked Canberra. Although I'd like to think there must have been some far less random and more carefully calculated basis to the thought process behind it.

The journey through the countryside or 'bush' as the Aussies refer to it was amazing. The roads are well maintained and open and although it's not mountainous, the view all around is of green, wide-open spaces. They also have very odd names for places, such as Wollongong, Ulladulla and Bundanoon but that naturally comes from the influence of the indigenous Aborigines.

Our driver also had the most amazing sixth sense for anything nature based and could spot a ring-tailed possum or a sunbathing python with unnerving accuracy for a man who was supposed to be watching the road. But I have to admit, for me, the highlight of the 'spot the Aussie animal' game wasn't a koala, wallaby or a wombat, but the kangaroo. I was ridiculously overexcited when we saw our first kangaroo bouncing through what was effectively someone's backyard. It just sat there, like a dog that belonged to the owners, and then hopped off to join its mate.

Once we had seen one, we saw loads and they were hilarious to watch. They are really quite large creatures with great long feet and little dangly arms just sort of lolloping about. Sometimes they look like overgrown squirrels, sometimes stretched out like dogs, but most of the time they looked like no other animal I'd ever seen before – as my two hundred and fifty photos of them clearly show.

Our base for the first night on the road was to be the Karoonda Park ranch near a place called Gelantipy. We were told on arrival that the ranch was closing the following day due to the fast approach of the raging bush fires only fifty kilometres away and that one hundred and thirty-five firemen would be using the ranch as a base to fight the fires. We had seen the thick smog rising over the tree line in the distance as we drove that day, but hadn't appreciated quite how close the fires were. The fire apparently started due to lightening striking the already dry land and had rapidly spread throughout the outskirts of Canberra. We later found out that about 70 per cent of the pastures, forests and national parks in the area were destroyed and more than five hundred homes were damaged.

The ranch was set in acres of sprawling forest and farmland and was beautifully rugged. We had the run of the land for the evening and for some reason that I'm still not entirely sure of to this day, I found myself agreeing to go cattle herding on horseback, with a few of the people we'd met on the bus.

I'm not a great fan of horses, but for no other reason than the fact they are huge, can run fast and I never feel entirely comfortable that I know how to control one when I'm sitting on it. My greatest fear in the world though is of a much smaller creature and one that I know I'm not alone in loathing. I don't even like the word 'spider' - it sounds creepy and the thought of them is sometimes enough to make me flinch and start to look around nervously.

I am so irrationally scared of spiders that when I first told my friends and family that I was going to Australia, it was the one thing they teased me about and the one thing that secretly filled me with dread. I'm not sure I ever went to a public toilet without checking under the seat first for the redbacks that are rumoured to lurk there and I actively avoided going to places I knew would be my idea of arachnophobia hell.

So, I need to set the scene as we started to make our way out to the cattle. There were six of us on horseback, three of us travellers and three ranch hands. We rode into the paddock which lead to the ranch land beyond and closed the gate behind us so we could regroup before going through the next gate into the pastures. I was second from the front, with my guide on her horse just in front of me, so the back of her horse was just alongside the front of mine. Just as she started to make conversation and I answered her question about what I do back home by telling her I am a police officer, I heard someone behind ask her, 'What's that on the back of your horse?'

As I glanced to the backside of her horse, just a few feet away from my leg, I saw a big, grey hairy Huntsman spider the size of the palm of my hand and I swear I could see it breathing! About a hundred things flew through my mind at the speed of light at that point and all of them were fuelled by wild panic. I considered the possibility that the horse's tail would flick it at me, it would somehow be able to jump at me, or that the guide who was turning to look at it, would dismissively flick it away in my direction because she would probably think nothing of it as a native Aussie, being used to huge spiders. So I started to scream.

41

The next thing I was aware of was sitting on my horse facing completely the opposite direction we had been facing. The guide was off her horse, standing beside me with a look of stunned horror on her face and she was stroking my hand telling me I was okay and to breathe slower. I was shaking with fear and sobbing uncontrollably, while everyone else was staring at me in shocked silence. I hadn't a clue what to say or what to do to diffuse the situation and all I could think about was the last thing I had said to her before I'd blanked out. So I stifled my sobs and tried to explain between gasps that I'd never had to arrest a spider!

The Great Ocean Road

We moved on from the fast-approaching smoke of the bush fires and hit the road to Melbourne. I had loved Sydney and there seems to be an underlying competition between the two cities, so I felt that Melbourne would have to be pretty special. Unfortunately we didn't really have much time there that night, but I did manage to return at the end of my trip before I flew home and it is a beautiful city.

Melbourne seems to be more open and greener than Sydney, with certain suburbs right on the coast and is home to long sandy beaches and manicured parks. There is a very relaxed and cosmopolitan feel to the city, which has a river running through the centre and is lined by restaurants and cafes. I also visited the Shrine of Remembrance, which was very moving with inscriptions and dedications to all those who had sacrificed their lives for their countries.

I did like Melbourne and would recommend it as somewhere to chill out and enjoy the relaxed atmosphere while still being in a large city. But, I confess I was still seduced by the Opera House, Harbour Bridge and energy of Sydney and it remains my favourite of the two cities. Although, the ten-year-old inside me could well have been swayed if I'd had the time to take the *Neighbours* TV set official tour in Melbourne, but I guess I'll never know.

We hit the road again after Melbourne and headed to the part of the journey on the South coast that I had been looking forward to the most. The Great Ocean Road was built by returned servicemen as a memorial to fellow servicemen who had been killed in the First

World War. It is 151 miles (243 kilometres) long and boasts some of the most stunningly beautiful coastline and coastal features I've ever seen.

The coastline is so rugged and sculpted, with so many stunning views along its entirety that you could spend the whole journey stopping to take photographs if you wanted to. So when we were given the option to take a helicopter ride over a section called the Twelve Apostles, I took the opportunity and it was breathtaking.

Driving in Australia is a feat in itself, with the vast distances between cities and towns and the amount of different time zones you cross as you travel. It was difficult to keep track of whether you should be having breakfast or going to bed sometimes. There were also plenty of amusing quirks along the way, such as road signs for skiing kangaroos, or skateboarding wombats, plenty of genuine wildlife to be spotted and a bizarre fascination with oversized Aussie landmarks at tourist sights. We managed to spot a fifty foot koala, a gigantic shrimp and a freakishly large pineapple – all very random.

The bus journey was also a great chance to meet people and make friends along the way and it's amazing how you can strike up conversations with complete strangers so easily when you're travelling. Although when I say easily, it's not always quite that simple.

One of the friends I made while on the south coast was a Japanese girl, who also happened to be deaf. I speak absolutely no Japanese and she spoke no English, although she could read and write English very well. Needless to say our conversations weren't exactly free flowing, but we clicked somehow and found our own way of communicating. I was really inspired by her and how brave she was to be travelling completely alone, not only in a country where she couldn't speak the language but when she couldn't even hear everything that we take so much for granted.

The bus journey along the south coast ended at Adelaide and we were shattered. In hindsight, I would have left myself a little more time and stayed there for a few days to recover from the intense week of travelling. However, that's why it's called hindsight and without the benefit of knowing any different, we had already booked ourselves on a flight to central Australia the following day to do Ayers Rock.

So, in preparation for another early start and thousands of miles of travel, we went out in Adelaide, drank far too much and ended up in a kebab shop at midnight with some apparently famous ex-cricketer. I say apparently, because sport never was my strong point and after wondering why the guy I was chatting to kept attracting people who wanted to shake his hand and say hello, Andy told me it was Dean Jones. That was the point I realised I'd better leave before I embarrassed myself. Right before I noticed I'd already spilled kebab sauce all down my front.

Red centre, big rock

The flight to Alice Springs from Adelaide takes two hours and for the majority of the entire journey all you can see is predominantly flat, red brown earth. Temperatures reach over forty degrees in the summer months and there are towns where the people live permanently underground during the daytime, in sophisticated caves they have bored out of the earth just to avoid the sun.

Alice Springs is the hottest place I have been ever before and ever since. There is literally no shade outside and it seems as if the sun is concentrated solely on the centre of Australia. The earth is still red there and the streets have very few trees or plants other than cactus and very adaptable hardcore plants that need little water.

One real shame about the Australians is the disappointing way they have historically treated the Aborigines. It is nowhere more apparent than on the streets of Alice Springs where they gather in groups, drunkenly intimidating people and begging for money to fund their drug and alcohol habits. In recent years, the Australian Government enforced modern cultural lifestyles on the Aborigines by offering them financial rewards in return for commitments such as ensuring their children attend school. Unfortunately, as a result, more recent Aborigine generations have turned to drug and alcohol abuse and have not been appropriately supported or encouraged to embrace their heritage.

We stayed overnight in a hostel, which had a poor excuse for a swimming pool, a pathetic air conditioning system, but thankfully enough cold beer for everyone. In fact, that seems to be the one thing you can guarantee at even the most remote Aussie bars in the middle of the outback. The toilets may be dodgy, the air con might only just work and the hope of getting a mobile phone signal or roadside assistance is almost non-existent, yet somehow they always have a well-stocked fridge of cold beer.

Our journey to Ayers Rock the following day started at 5.00 am for a five-hour bus drive to the centre via Kings Canyon. Kings Canyon is how I envisage the Grand Canyon would be, but on a much smaller scale. It was incredibly hot, very rugged and hard going climbing and walking in the heat.

We arrived at Ayers Rock in time to claim our camping ground, have a barbeque and make our way to the rock for sunset. Ayers Rock is a UNESCO World Heritage site, known as Uluru to the indigenous people. It is a sacred spiritual site. Unfortunately, like Niagara Falls, it hasn't escaped commercialism and there were no less than nine resorts when I visited, not to mention the numerous campsites. But, I have to admit that their existence is not an imposition and somehow, the natural integrity of the site has been preserved.

One of the main attractions of visiting Ayers Rock is to watch the changing colours of the rock at sunset and sunrise and I was looking forward to something amazing. Unfortunately though, when you envisage such an event, you don't allow for the several hundred other tourists who've also gathered for the experience. Needless to say, it was hardly a private or emotional spectacle and although a sunset in the desert is never going to wholly disappoint, I have to say I was decidedly unmoved.

For one thing, the lights from the hotels in the vicinity don't make for an unaffected night sky. But more puzzling was the fact that due to the position of the designated viewing areas you are forced to watch either a large rock in the middle of the desert, or a sun setting or rising, but not as the guide books would have you believe, both simultaneously.

We spent the night sleeping alfresco in heavy duty sleeping bags, which I had one of the lads check and double check, at least three times to avoid a repeat and unwanted experience with anything eight legged.

After the equally uninspiring sunrise, we walked around the base of the rock and noticed that you are only permitted to take photographs at certain points around the perimeter. This is to honour and respect the spiritual beliefs of the Aborigines, who own the site and the reason they request that visitors refrain from climbing the rock. Naturally, human nature isn't all that respectful a lot of the time and plenty of tourists do make the arduous trek to the summit, despite a number of deaths every year. Not only is the face totally exposed, very steep and prone to strong winds, but also other than a very simple chain to hold on to for those both ascending and descending, there are absolutely no safety precautions and you climb at your own risk.

I don't really class myself as a spiritual person, but having seen the damage already inflicted on the indigenous Australians and not wanting to tempt the fate of an antagonised Aboriginal God, I decided against the climb. To be entirely honest, the option was taken away from us, as with temperatures over thirty degrees by 8.30 am, the rock was off limits for climbing anyway, but I'd like to think I would still have decided against it.

Cairns

The heat in Australia so far, although intense in places had been fairly dry, however in Cairns it was a completely different experience. The moment we stepped off the plane, we were hit by a wall of stiflingly humid heat, which grabs the back of your throat and engulfs you. It feels like there is no air and no release from the sun.

Cairns itself is like a coastal backpackers' paradise and the first place in Australia so far that I'd felt was almost entirely devoted to tourism. Wherever we went there were bars, cafes and restaurants with offers for backpackers to eat cheaply, hostels with competitive rates and gimmicks to attract custom, and plenty of activities and tours both day and night.

The town is right on the coast and with the Great Barrier Reef just off the mainland, one of the main draws to the area is scuba diving. Before visiting Cairns, I had already decided to dive there, but on arriving I felt the need for a day off. It seems ridiculous to talk about wanting time to relax, when essentially I was on the holiday of a lifetime, but with so much to do in such a vast country, I was constantly on the go.

There are plenty of ways to travel, depending on what you want to do and what sort of trip you choose to have. I know plenty of people who have worked their way around different countries, some successfully managing to see everything they wanted and others who became stuck in one city, partying their hard-earned cash away and forgetting why they went there in the first place. Then there are those that prefer to travel for only a few weeks at a time to fewer destinations and relax into it.

But for me, it seems that no matter how much or how little time I have anywhere, I tend to pack as much as I physically can into my time and find myself going into minor meltdown every so often, in need of some time out.

That was my intention in Cairns, until we were told there was a cyclone on the way and if we didn't go diving the following day, we would risk having to wait for up to a week for the storms to pass and the conditions to suitably settle. There are so many dive schools in Cairns and absolutely no shortage of options, whether you are an experienced diver or a complete novice. I'll elaborate on the diving later, but suffice it to say I was pleased I dived before the storm, while the conditions were good.

I spent the next few days finally relaxing around Cairns and visiting some very tranquil places in the surrounding area. The Atherton Tablelands is a lush mountain plain with beautiful waterfalls and forests, dating back far longer than the country has been inhabited. Part of my tour also included the serene beauty of Paronella Park - a Spanish-style garden initially built as a private haven by a Spaniard in the 1930s for his new wife, but later opened to the public.

My only other pastime was shopping and sleeping and I loved it. There wasn't a great deal to shop for apart from tourist trinkets and keepsakes, but just to be on my own for a couple of days and have nowhere in particular to travel to was wonderful.

My friend Andy, with whom I'd been travelling until that point had taken a few days to go to Cape Tribulation in the northern rainforests, which is somewhere many people make the effort to visit in the tropics. People that is who don't freak out and lose all sense of reality when faced with spiders four times bigger than the one I'd encountered in the south. I'd decided long before that the experience of being faced with another spider of any significant proportion would most likely tip me over the edge and that I'd be far better avoiding even the slightest possibility.

To end my two days off, I sat with my book and ate in a little restaurant with tables outside and a waiter who seemed to make it his mission to make conversation with me so I wouldn't feel alone. It was quite sweet of him really, but when I want a Shirley Valentine moment, I like to be left to it and revel in the luxury of being totally unsociable.

Unfortunately, later that evening, I received the sad news that my Nan had passed away at home and I was devastated. I felt totally alone and in desperate need to be with my family, so the following day I left Australia for England.

It was a sad time and I spent a couple of weeks at home, being with my family and saying goodbye to my Nan. I eventually returned to Australia to continue my travels with the full encouragement and support of my family. However, my brief return to the UK meant that for the rest of my journey around Australia, I would be travelling alone.

Going solo

When I said goodbye to my parents at Heathrow airport for my return to Cairns, I felt incredibly overwhelmed. I felt such a range of emotions about being on my own, from apprehension and anticipation to pride and exhilaration, but most of all I felt an amazing sense of freedom.

My journey via Singapore was somewhat eventful. During the night, a Japanese woman who had spent a notable amount of time on the loo had a bit of an 'episode' next to my seat. From the distinctively unpleasant stench as she passed my aisle seat I gathered she'd had an unfortunate accident and watched unamused as she (in my opinion) feigned passing out, probably from sheer embarrassment, right next to me.

I'm a little ashamed to admit that when the steward who rushed to the woman's aide asked me to vacate my seat for her, my first thought was of the mess she would make on my chair, should I have to subsequently return to it! I am probably a horrible person, but I shuffled and lingered, all the time secretly suspecting from her bad acting that she was faking and fortunately her daughter insisted she go back with her to their seats much farther along the cabin.

Still, after being diverted to Sydney due to a storm in Brisbane, I was eventually upgraded to first class for the last leg of the journey and spent the next six hours in relative luxury and most certainly minus any incontinent strangers.

On arrival back in Cairns, I made my way straight to the hostel I had stayed in prior to going home. Many of the hostels in Australia (and similarly as I later found out in New Zealand) consist of multiple occupancy rooms, with a number of bunk beds and you can specify ether mixed or single gender dorms. I had decided to stay in female-only dorms from then on after a rather graphic experience in a rather small, mixed room during my first few days in Cairns. I'll spare the detail, but suffice it to say the guy on the opposite bunk had drunkenly brought a girl back with him and I woke up only feet away from a graphic display you should never have to witness that close up.

I checked in, collected my key and took my bags to the six-person dorm to claim a bed and dump my bags. As I walked into the room, I came face to face with the very same deaf girl I had said goodbye to in Adelaide over three weeks before. I could hardly believe it and we were both so pleased to see a familiar face.

I soon learned from my journey around Australia that it is an unbelievably easy country to travel and you are never alone for long. There are basically two routes around eastern Australia, which incorporate the same destinations in a circuit either clockwise or anti-clockwise. Therefore, as I discovered several times, you invariably cross paths with the same groups of people at numerous different locations even when you think you have seen the last of them days, or even weeks, before.

I left Cairns and my new friend after a few more days and travelled south to one of my favourite places on the east coast, Mission Beach. I didn't really have any plans there and there wasn't really much to do but relax. The beach was a long stretch of pale sand, lined with palm trees and unbelievably deserted.

I immediately met a group of girls in the hostel and we cracked open the cheap wine while we cooked that night. The hostels are incredibly sociable, with communal kitchens and dormitories, so you can't help but meet people and compare travelling stories and experiences. The hostel in Mission Beach had an open kitchen and was surrounded by tropical plants and palms, which meant that we had all sorts of bugs and creatures crawling and flying about most nights, including the odd gecko.

After a few nights relaxing, losing a drunken pool competition against a rather dodgy Aussie in questionable white PVC pants and not being able to swim in the sea due to stinging jellyfish, I left Mission Beach. I made vague plans to meet up with the girls I'd met a few stops down the line and took a boat to Magnetic Island.

The island isn't particularly dazzling, but again just a very relaxing place, rugged beaches and the gateway to one of Australia's best dive sites – the Yongala Wreck. I planned to spend a day or two exploring the island, relaxing and then do the dive. Although it was a bit of a financial toss-up between more diving and sky diving, which I'd also promised myself I'd do at some point, should I have the bottle.

As it was, I never did get to do the wreck because the torrential rain each night made the conditions horrendous and not worth the effort. In fact, the weather didn't exactly make Magnetic Island my best experience on the whole as it turned out, although if I'm honest my own ignorance didn't help matters. There is a very long, very secluded path you can walk on the island, which is supposed to be a koala trail, so named because of the apparent high likelihood of spotting koalas. I decided to do the uphill hike on the cloudiest, muggiest, overcast day and therefore very foolishly decided against wearing any sunscreen.

The path led uphill very gradually, through quite overgrown bush and rocky terrain and, quite unnervingly, there were very few other people along the way, not to mention a distinct absence of koalas. So there I was with no sun protection, very little water and acutely aware of every little crack of a twig or rustling of leaves and scaring myself with overdramatic thoughts of being attacked before I dehydrated. I finally got to the top and with dismay, found two rather decrepit, deserted look-out structures made of dry stone and rather too closely resembling something out of *The Blair Witch Project*.

I have no idea looking back, what possessed me to do that walk on my own, nor why having reached the eerie summit, I decided to have my packed lunch on a precarious rock with my back to the 'Blair Witch shelter', but I can only think it's because sometimes when you're travelling, you get a bit seduced by the whole experience and tend to do things you probably wouldn't consider doing if you were at home.

Still, having survived without attack by witches, axe murderers or depraved koalas I made my way back considerably faster than I'd come and started to feel the effects of the overcast, yet apparently deceptively strong, sun. By bedtime I was only a couple of shades lighter than a ripe tomato and my face, neck and shoulders were so sore I thought I might be permanently scarred. At this point, I would like to advocate what I firmly believe is the miracle curing power of aloe vera gel.

Yachts and dingoes

Before we'd gone our separate ways, Andy who is a very keen yachtsman and all-round sailing type had impressed on me the benefits of taking a trip on a yacht around the Whitsunday Islands. So, left to my own devices and trusting in his knowledgeable experience, I went to Airlie Beach and booked myself on the sleekest-looking, fastest yacht I could find.

I then spent the next three days slicing through waves on an 85-foot boat, which spent most of the time at a forty-five degree angle causing everyone to cling on for dear life. We couldn't talk due to the wind and we couldn't take any pictures because we needed to hold on with both hands.

To top it off, the skipper then made sudden decisions to change course randomly, resulting in everyone having to somehow grab a piece of equipment or rope and 'tack' or 'jibe' or whatever it's called, which apparently gave us all the chance to experience 'real sailing'. Quite frankly, I'd have been considerably happier prone on a triple-decked cruiser, with waiter service and minimum physical exertion. But then I'm not and never have been much of a sailor.

Other than the obvious drawbacks, I have to admit that the living conditions on the yacht were very comfortable. The islands were worth a visit, although not the idyllic paradise I was hoping for because I think they've been over visited by tourists. We also managed to do some snorkelling, although due to the season's influx of stinging micro jellyfish we had to wear rather fetching, all-over Lycra bodysuits, which did take the edge off somewhat.

After a welcome return to dry land, I made my way to Hervey Bay to get ready for my next scheduled trip, camping on Fraser Island. Pretty much every backpacker who travels the east coast of Oz does

Fraser Island and it really is a fantastic experience. There are only about three hundred inhabitants on the island and hardly any proper roads, because most land is either dirt track covered in sand, or sand tracks of varying depth.

All driving is done in four-wheel drive trucks, most sleeping in tents and no swimming is done in the sea, unless you fancy a brief and fatal encounter with a tiger shark. The beaches on Fraser Island are beautiful – white sands stretching for miles and the inland lakes are absolutely stunning blue.

As the tour company provides vehicles, tents and camping gear, they divide everyone into small groups and send you on your way with a truck, basic instructions for how to drive it and tips for what to do if any of the numerous dingoes on the island take an interest in you.

The island's tracks are only single lane and are riddled with potholes, steep slopes and so much sand it's like driving on snow. The truck's gearshift varies depending on whether the sand is soft or compact and if you meet anyone coming in the opposite direction it's pretty much a free for all. Of the nine people in my group only five were able to drive and surprisingly no one wanted to go first, except me.

Once I got my head around the gears, it was great fun and such a rush revving up the sandbanks like a crazed rally driver. There were plenty of dunes where we literally had to empty everyone out of the truck to stop it sinking and plenty where no one could get their trucks up the slopes at all, except me.

Now I'd like to profess a skill for artful off-roading, but if I'm totally honest I have to confess my success was a combination of criss-crossing for traction, going like a bat out of hell, while over-revving the engine in first because it wasn't mine and sheer luck. Everyone wanted me to drive and I actually felt like Lewis Hamilton, until I misjudged what turned out to be a rather large sand dune and took off, causing everyone to smack their heads on the roof of the truck, except me!

We spent two nights camping on the dunes while keeping one eye out for dingoes and washing in the rock pools while keeping one eye out for sharks. I was with a group of total strangers and the different groups met up to camp together each night, so I ended up meeting so many new people. It really is a fabulous experience and the white beaches and turquoise lakes are like a little bit of paradise. Paradise that is, if you can manage to get up early enough in the morning to experience them before the arrival of truckloads of other backpackers.

Push the bush!

After my diving plans had fallen through on Magnetic Island, I had been thinking a lot about doing a sky dive. I know it's something that can be done anywhere really, but it was considerably cheaper in Oz and one of the many things that you seem to get carried away with doing as part of the whole travelling experience.

I had a brief stopover in Noosa before arriving in Brisbane for a few days, where I managed to find a skydiving company I liked the sound of. The drop zone turned out to be nearer Noosa than Brisbane, but they offered a pickup and return to Brisbane and a night's accommodation in with the package, so I opted for that and started to get nervous.

On the morning of the big day, I was picked up at the hostel along with a couple of guys I'd met who were also doing the jump and off we went. I kind of half expected an airport or at least some sort of presentable airstrip building and dormitory, but as the roads got more deserted we eventually pulled up to what looked like an old corrugated iron shed with a landing strip.

Almost everyone there was male. Most of them looked like they hadn't seen a woman in months and the accommodation turned out to be a mattress on the floor in a communal sleeping area. I started to wonder what I had let myself in for. Before long, it was clear they weren't the woman-deprived bunch of crazy adrenalin junkies I'd feared, they were just adrenalin junkies and on the whole, thoroughly nice people.

I met my tandem sky dive trainer and cursed myself for telling him what I did for a living, when his apparent amused interest made me wonder if he'd spent too much time on the wrong side of the law and was plotting some sort of revenge.

We went through the procedure for exiting the plane and I got kitted up with my suit and tandem harness. I was told to remember to cross my arms at the door of the plane, lean my head back onto his shoulder with my eyes open and push my pelvis out as we jumped. As we fell I would have to keep my head up, arch my back slightly and open my arms wide, while keeping my legs behind me and my feet apart.

I figured that seeing as I was attached to him, the getting out of the door bit wasn't in question and as long as I opened my eyes so as not to waste the experience, the rest would pretty much work itself out. We went through the drill on the plane before take-off where he told me that as long as I crossed my arms and kept my pelvis forward or 'push the bush' as he cheekily put it, he'd do the rest.

By the time the plane took off, I was quite frankly bricking it. There were five of us squashed into what appeared to be an exceptionally small plane. One guy was doing his final qualifying jump for his accelerated freefall (AFF) course, I had opted for a video recording of the jump, so we had a camera man, my trainer, me and of course the pilot.

As we climbed higher and higher, I was doing my best impression of a calm person on the outside, but verging on the brink of hysteria inside. I get inappropriately giggly when I get nervous and whenever I look back at the video, the ridiculous nervous grin on my face mixed with sheer terror, reminds me instantly how I was feeling during that whole flight.

At about 9,000 feet, the other sky diver opened the door and the most unbelievably loud rush of air thundered into the cabin and he jumped, just like that. I was just catching my breath from the shock of an open doorway and no seatbelts, when the plane suddenly banked and started to climb back up for our jump. At that point, I had lost all feeling of the giggles and while I pressed myself as close to the inside of the plane as I could to avoid the still, wide-open doorway, the reality started to dawn.

Before I knew it, the trainer was asking if I was ready and edging us forward. I had absolutely no idea if I wanted to jump at all, but it was going to happen anyway so I closed my eyes, crossed my arms and pushed the bush!

I can't remember the instant I actually left the plane because I think fear momentarily blanked it out, but I do remember turning in the air and then looking down with the ground 12,000 feet below. It was absolutely the most amazing, exhilarating rush I have ever experienced in my life. The free fall is 200 feet per second, but it doesn't feel scary, or like you're tumbling out of the sky to your imminent death as I'd imagined. It is the most fantastic feeling and the only reason you feel like you're falling is because you can see things on the ground getting gradually clearer.

I think I may have let out the odd girlie squeal and more than a couple of words my mother wouldn't have approved of, but all with a huge grin on my face and this time not through petrified hysteria.

When the chute opened, I took control of the guide lines and had a go at twirling us around slowly at first and then faster, until I actually felt a bit sick and remembered I was the one making it spin. Then we had the most gentle, uneventful landing and I literally couldn't speak for grinning and giggling like an excited child. I was quite literally buzzing from the rush and willing there and then to forfeit the rest of my travels and sign up for the AFF course myself.

I was so grateful for the accommodation at the drop zone because when you jump out of a plane for the very first time, the only thing you want to talk about for the next few hours is jumping out of a plane. We had a barbeque, plenty of cold beers and swapped experiences and stories about life and jumping out of planes for the rest of the night. Then I went to sleep still grinning.

Off the beaten track

Backpacking is one of the most fabulously liberating experiences because you can decide where you go and how long for as you go along and you meet so many different people. However, the reasons it is so much fun, the good times, full on travelling and non-stop socialising can also get a little overwhelming if you're like me and need your space from time to time.

I had a brief stopover in Byron Bay on the east coast for St Patrick's Day and ended up in a hostel next to a stagnant pond, with too many cobwebs and a toilet I tried not to use for two days. I met a couple of girls there and had a few too many shots of a drink I can't remember how to make, before I started to feel like I needed a break from the backpacking scene.

So I decided to visit a small place called Lennox Head, recommended to me by a friend who'd been there previously and took a local bus off the beaten track. When I got to Lennox Head, to my satisfaction, there was only one hostel in the town and none of the usual cafes and bars bursting with cheap deals to attract backpackers.

I booked into the hostel for three nights and after the first night had the four-man dorm to myself. I decided to keep myself to myself and made minimal conversation with a few people in the kitchen while cooking dinner, before retreating to my bed early with a good book. It might sound dull to some people but three days of solitude was pure bliss to me and I loved every second.

My days consisted of getting up when I felt like it and having a cup of tea and breakfast before packing my towel, camera, sunscreen, water and book and heading for the beach. I walked past a beautiful tea tree lake on the way each morning, which I possibly would have swam in if it hadn't looked exactly like cold tea. Then I'd find my usual secluded spot on the almost deserted beach and settle down for the rest of the morning and early afternoon. I surfaced only for a swim now and again and then when I felt hungry, I'd pack up and go to one of the many beachside cafes and sit with my lunch and read some more.

Sometimes I walked, sometimes I browsed the few little shops in the limited town and sometimes I just sat and revelled in not making conversation or being in the slightest bit sociable. It was my idea of heaven. Then, after three days, I decided I was rested and ready to be back among people again. As I got ready to leave, I chatted to a girl who was travelling in the opposite direction to me and had come from an interesting little town just south of where I was. There wasn't a great deal more to Bellingen than Lennox Head, but apparently it was a friendly little hippy town, with a few more cafes and tourist attractions and a particular hostel with an intriguing difference.

I decided to pay this hostel a visit for one night and check out the curious tale I had been told about its resident photographer. Apparently a very talented, slightly hippy photographer lodged at the hostel rent-free, in exchange for taking pictures of guests completely naked – who wouldn't want to at least go and have a look?

I was soon standing looking at the hostel's huge display wall of hundreds of photographs of men, women, couples and groups, all totally starkers. They weren't sordid in any way though, which was the gimmick. Each one was very artfully shot at either a tasteful angle, or with the use of props to conceal any private areas. Some were artistic, some comical but all were fabulous pictures and I was very tempted.

That night, I went for a few beers with some people from the hostel and with a little Dutch courage, got talking photography with the hippy artist. It turned out that he had a few photos left on the reel he needed to process the next day and if I wanted, I could be his last strip.

I guess I'd known I would do it before I even got on the bus the day before. I had that same excited and slightly nervous feeling I always got when I knew I was about to do something anyway, even though I knew I probably shouldn't.

The following morning I got up very early and set off in the hippy photographer's truck to a remote Australian location, with no phone, no one but the two of us and no idea how I would justify myself should I be found half-dead and penniless if he decided to rob and attack me, given that I'd provided him with the perfect opportunity should he chose to.

However, fuelled by my ethos 'you only live once', I made small talk and tried not to contemplate the bizarreness of what I was doing, which always helps. We arrived at a beautifully tranquil river, surrounded by drooping trees and I started to get the giggles. As I stood awkwardly watching the hippy unload his camera gear I shifted uncomfortably and looked around, trying to wonder what I should do. Then, without even looking up and with about as much interest as if I'd been a bowl of fruit, he told me to take my clothes off and I did.

I can't really explain how it felt to be there, in the open air with a total stranger, completely naked, but I don't think anyone would believe me if I said it felt strangely normal and not at all sexual. I felt totally comfortable after a couple of minutes; once I was reassured it was all about getting the right photo. Although, when I say totally comfortable, that doesn't account for the fact that I was mentally counting up the body parts I wished were smaller, firmer, higher, leaner etc and wishing I hadn't done quite so much good living during the past two months.

My private photo shoot began in the river. Well, it was actually all in the river, but the positions varied. I wasn't keen on the wicker chair shot with me leaning over the back staring at the camera, too tacky. For the next one, I had to lay on my back in the shallow water with my arms across my chest, my leg slightly crossed and the camera behind my shoulder, which was better but very cold. But my favourite shot was on the other side of the river in the rapid water with the white water around my hips and my arms crossed over my chest, totally bare, but totally tasteful.

We didn't have more than three shots and I probably would have liked another few choices of my favourite pose, but I settled for the one I had and left Bellingen feeling totally liberated, with my little secret safely stored away.

Homeward bound

My last two weeks in Australia went fairly quickly and relatively uneventfully. I wanted to visit Newcastle on the east coast for sentimental reasons, after studying at Newcastle upon Tyne University in the UK and living there for many years, it seemed appropriate to visit the Oz version. Unfortunately, Australians don't have a patch on the Geordies and the Newcastle down under, is considerably duller than its English namesake.

I don't think it helped that I arrived on a Sunday, when it was mostly closed, it was raining and overcast and frankly quite cold. Unfortunately the hostel I picked had all the downsides of some of the grottier student accommodation I had long ago gladly left behind.

I returned to Sydney for a last few days on Bondi beach, browsing the markets and catching up with the friends I had stayed with on my arrival two months before. The final leg of my journey was a bus trip to Melbourne to spend some time in the city, having only had one night there on my last visit.

I felt like I had missed most of Melbourne and I wanted to give it a real chance before I left. I wandered round the centre for a few days, shopping, visiting the supposedly haunted city gaol and the very moving war memorials and then went further out to the trendy area of St Kilda.

I think if I'd have been there with friends, I'd have loved St Kilda and Melbourne more, but I didn't really get to see the nightlife or have the energy to explore any more. I think by that time I had exhausted my backpacking enthusiasm, for a while at least and was ready for the journey home.

I can't choose between my favourite places in Australia. It is such a beautiful, friendly country and so wonderfully accessible to travel. I can't illustrate enough how easy it is to explore as a single traveller, nor can I recommend it enough. There is something so amazingly exhilarating about being able to go where you want, when you want, being able to do what you want and having only yourself to answer to and you can be as sociable or as solitary as you chose. But however you do it; you definitely, without doubt, have to be prepared to throw caution to the wind every now and again.

Sally Wootton

Greenland 1992

The ice scattered fjord, Greenland

Coming in to Nanortalik,

Fishing, Greenland style

My first icebergs

Greenland 1992

Me, waist deep, digging the shit pit!

Base camp, what a backdrop.

Bathing in glacier meltwater and quite literally freezing.

Our first taste of snow camping

A breathtaking view of our arctic home

The 1988 Olympic bob sleigh run at Calgary

The Capilano suspension bridge, Vancouver

Elk - or caribou, Banff

Sandcastles at Harrison Hot Springs

Canada 2000

Mountie moose, Toronto

Shark moose and high dive moose, Toronto

Rainbow over Niagara Falls

No introduction necessary! Sydney

Kangaroo!

Push the bush!

Giant Koala

How cute? Koala at the
Australia Zoo

The Seahorse, Great Ocean Road,

Australia 2003

Camel riding in Alice Springs

The Great Ocean Road

Insert your own caption!

Emu and the Oz Experience bus

The 'smile' of Ayers Rock

South East Asia 2004

A Buddhist monk enjoys a rare solitary moment at Angkor Wat, Cambodia

Market day, Luang Prabang, Laos

How many people on one bike? Cambodia

An odd performance, Luang Prabang, Laos

A very packed tuk-tuk, Bangkok

Bridge over the River Kwai, Thailand

South East Asia 2004

Kanchanaburi, Thailand

One of the traditional locals, Vietnam

I wouldn't have been so brave if it had eight legs!
Bangkok

Feeling very
sorry for myself
after my accident
on Koh Tao

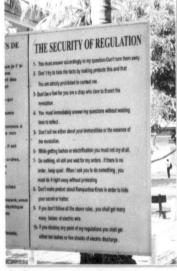

THE SECURITY OF REGULATION

The chilling rules of S-21, Phnom Penh

A cell at the genocide museum,
Phnom Penh, Cambodia

Campfire with the Karen tribe, Thailand

The border Thailand - Cambodia

Angkor Wat, Cambodia

Wat face?! Angkor

The Grand Palace, Bangkok

So happy to be crossing a border at last!

South East Asia 2004

Our boat on the 'Perfume river'
Hue, Vietnam

The sign at the door of the Dead Fish Tower Cafe, Siem Reap, Cambodia

The floating markets, Bangkok

Emma and me on Christmas Day, Koh Tao, Thailand

The Mekong River into Laos

The Killing Fields, Cambodia

Those dreaded steps of Angkor Wat

Chiang Mai, Thailand

70

Southeast Asia 2004 - 2005

Falling in love ... with Bangkok

When things don't turn out the way you expect them to and you feel a bit lost or down, it's sometimes a good time to have a spring clean, get a new hair cut, or have a bit of a blow out with the credit card. That's usually the time I start to think about travelling again.

In 2003 I decided I would save up and plan a trip to Southeast Asia, taking in Thailand, Laos, Cambodia and Vietnam and then go to New Zealand. I was renting at the time and put all my spare cash into the trip, which I decided I'd start in November 2004 for about four months or so. I planned a route from Thailand, through to Laos at its northern border point and then to Vietnam and south to Cambodia before coming back to Thailand. I had a couple of friends who also wanted to travel and I would do Asia with one and then meet another in New Zealand. It all fell into place and I couldn't wait for the journey to start.

Toward the end of the year before I left, I'd had a pretty full on and stressful time at work and was exhausted. So by the time I got to Bangkok I was so tired and relieved to be away that it took me a couple of days to relax and rejuvenate myself. I remember getting the cab from the airport and feeling totally dazed as I sat in the back looking out at the buildings and the city as we drove to the hotel.

I had booked a hotel for a week in Bangkok and had the first few days alone until my friend Emma joined me. When I arrived all I remember is the pungent smell in the air, which seemed to be stifling in the heat, and the rough, untidiness of the streets and the people begging on them.

I went to my room and stayed there sleeping, reading and getting my head clear for thirty-six hours solid. When I eventually emerged, I decided I'd better take note of the advice in the guidebooks, which recommended dressing conservatively and covering up your shoulders and ankles. So I dressed in a loose-fitting, long-sleeved top

71

and baggy pants and went down to breakfast. As I sat in the open-sided restaurant, I felt so proud of myself and so excited. Then I started to realise that the guidebooks hadn't given quite as true depiction of Thai culture as they possibly could have.

My hotel appeared to be in the heart of one of the sex districts of Bangkok and as I watched the scantily clad Thai girls (and some Thai boys) walk by, I realised I may be a touch overdressed.

The hotel had a roof terrace pool and bar and I decided that my first official day outside my hotel room would be spent soaking up the rays and breathing in the smog! That's one of the notable things about Bangkok, the thick permanent layer of pollution that hovers in the air like a blanket, from thousands of badly maintained car and bike exhausts.

Another noticeable feature of the city is the skyline. Not in the breathtaking, awe-inspiring New York skyline kind of a way, but more in a 'how can there be that many unfinished, part constructed sky scrapers in such close proximity?' kind of a way. As I lay by the pool trying not to think about the damage to my lungs, I counted at least three unfinished buildings towering over my relatively little hotel.

After several hours baking in the direct sun, I felt rested enough to brave the city streets and discovered that I loved Bangkok. The city is absolutely buzzing with activity. The streets are full of carts and stalls selling all types of 'food' and the whole place smells of something I couldn't quite put my finger on, mixed with peanut sauce. The kerbs are lined with people selling all manner of things from T-shirts, jewellery and other trinkets to noodles, corn on the cob or more exotic delicacies such as deep fried baby frog, sea horses or packets of locusts.

There are bars bursting with people drinking at all times of the day and girls dripping all over the European men who frequent certain areas of the city for entertainment. I knew that Thailand's sex industry is world renowned, but I still sort of expected it to go on behind closed doors and be a bit hush hush. I just couldn't get over how many old, fat, wrinkly white men there were blatantly dripping in tiny, overly made-up young Thai girls and I couldn't help but stare.

Not to mention the Thai women who were actually Thai men. There was something absolutely fascinating about these immaculately dressed, perfectly groomed guys with micro-minis clinging to their amazingly pert bums and legs up to their armpits. They had the clothes, the hair, the make-up and the killer heels – not to mention the meat and two veg and telltale Adams apple.

But the craziest thing about Bangkok is the sheer number of cars, taxis, motorbikes and tuk-tuks. I couldn't believe how many moving vehicles could cram into four lanes of road in such a busy city centre and at how recklessly they drive. There seems to be one rule in Bangkok when it comes to driving and that is to occupy any available space possible in a bid to get a little further along the road, while sounding your horn as loudly as possible.

I travelled the sky rail rather than brave the roads on my own on my first day of exploring and went all over several districts, becoming quite adept at fending off street sellers and navigating the crowds. I loved the hustle and bustle of the place and the infectious energy and couldn't wait for Emma to arrive so we could really get stuck in.

Same same, but different

When Emma arrived a few nights later we couldn't wait to go into town and catch up over a few cold beers. It was late by the time we made our way out and for such a vibrant city it was disappointing to discover that a lot of the bars closed around 1.00 am to try and calm the drinking culture down. But that doesn't mean there aren't plenty of places for late night drinking if you look closely enough.

We found a little street bar and stayed there for hours, catching up on the months we hadn't seen each other and enjoying being able to drink outside in the heat. By the time we made our way back to the hotel the streets were deserted, the night markets had long closed and we were just starting to resign ourselves to having to go to bed, when we saw the bar staff in the restaurant who seemed to be having a late night drink of their own.

So before long we were chatting and drinking and practising our very bad Thai while the sun started to rise and the somewhat tipsy staff set the tables for breakfast. I have no idea how much we drank that night, or what time we went to bed. But before we left, several local police units came into the restaurant to fill up before starting their day patrol and because we could, we had breakfast with them.

When we eventually surfaced and wandered into town, we decided to go to the infamous Koh San Road street market, where you can get anything you want at the right price, from fake designer bags, cheap Thai clothes, jewellery and CDs to driving licenses and passports.

Due to the volume of traffic in Bangkok and the inflated price for tourists, taxis are slow and expensive, so the most authentic and quickest way to travel is by tuk-tuk. If you've never experienced a Thai tuk-tuk then the best way to describe it is to imagine sitting in an open-sided, oversized disability car behind a slightly crazed driver who speaks poor English and takes pleasure in risking your life at surprising speed, while darting in and out of spaces you never think are going to be quite big enough. It's like the thrill of a slightly scary ride at one of those travelling fairs where you're never quite sure that health and safety is top priority, so you shut your eyes for the fast bits and hope for the best.

The other frustrating thing about tuk-tuk drivers is that they never take you directly to where you want to go. There is always a silk shop, or a café owned by one of their 'friends' which they will earnestly try to persuade you to enter on the basis they will get commission if you buy something. No amount of pleading or gentle persuasion will induce them to take you to the actual shop or café you want to go to and they will play ignorant and simply laugh it off while proclaiming, 'Same, same, but different!'

We soon learned that the only way to win their little game was to threaten to take a different tuk-tuk and if we felt particularly bold, throw their 'Same, same but different' exclamation back to them while pointing at the other ride. It soon got the point across and we were at the Koh San Road ready to shop.

Shopping in Thailand is an art in itself and everyone expects you to haggle. They have two pricing systems, one for locals and one for tourists, so you know that you can easily knock half the cost off as a starting point. It's a bit unnerving at first and the bottom line is you're actually arguing over a few pounds with people who earn less in a year than we do in one month. But that's the culture and once you get the hang of it, it's actually good fun. The Thai people have a wonderful cheeky sense of humour and will try their luck with almost anything to get a few extra Thai Baht out of you.

The wrong border

Our journey through Southeast Asia undoubtedly provided some of the most fabulous experiences of all my travels, but it also brought some of the worst bad luck. There seemed to be a point when a catalogue of things started to go wrong and our only options were to let them get us down, or to accept that shit happens and move on. So we developed a fabulous resilience by laughing ridiculously each time, at how we'd managed to somehow encounter yet another new crisis.

Things started to go wrong as we tried to leave Thailand. In the true spirit of travelling, we had booked two economy seats on the night train to the northern border with Laos at Chiang Mai and thought we'd travel south through Laos to Cambodia, return to Thailand for Christmas and then go on to Vietnam.

So we boarded the train and left Bangkok for the twelve-hour journey in the cheap seats. Our fears of being stuck on a cramped train with chickens and pigs and stifling heat were short-lived when we saw how clean and almost empty the train was. There were a few other backpackers on the train, great air conditioning and even waiter service with cold drinks and snacks. It couldn't have been better.

Until, that was, we left the train at about 6.00 am, having had very little sleep and realised that we were at the wrong border. We had, in fact, taken the completely wrong train and had no way of getting to the planned border entry unless we fancied another twelve-hour journey on another slow train. Excellent!

Still, we decided to make the most of it and opted to go across the border to Laos at Vientiane instead. So we hailed a small tuk-tuk and took the short ride to the border point, assuming the lack of other people around must be due to the time of day. When we arrived at the border, we were informed that not only was the border shut due to a rather inconveniently timed Asian World Summit meeting, but that there would be no way of entering at that point for several days. Oh how we laughed.

Anyone who's ever been to an Asian border town will know that there is generally very little there other than the border entry, visa control, possibly a bus or train exchange and some extortionately priced snack bars. After a hasty review of our predicament, we realised we had little choice than to make the return journey back through Thailand and go through to Cambodia instead.

It was at the dusty little border bus exchange that I had my first experience of Asian public toilets. Being a newcomer to the scene, I hadn't realised that if you are in a particularly well-catered for WC, then you have the option to pay a token fee for a sheet of toilet roll on the way in. If however, like me, you are not aware of this custom then you'll find yourself balancing precariously over a relatively small hole in the ground, trying to avoid splashing your own feet while cursing yourself for not knowing the Thai for 'Excuse me, is there any paper please?'

I think it's also worth adding that even in those facilities with porcelain surrounds and toilet paper, you still have to perform the balancing act of trying not to drape any displaced clothing in your predecessor's leftovers. The flushing method typically consists of varying forms of container to scoop and slosh water from a nearby bucket and if you happen upon a particularly basic loo, then it's just not worth even trying to breathe through your nose.

After much use of the international language of pointing at a map, pleading and pulling our best damsels in distress faces, we managed to get on a bus headed south. That is to say, we managed to get on a bus headed somewhere, that we had no choice but to hope was in the direction we wanted. The truth was, we managed to successfully navigate at least three bus changes during the twelve hours that followed and at each new exchange we had absolutely no idea whether we were getting on the right bus. The only reassurance we had was that because we were two of only three white people on the packed buses, we stood out like sore thumbs and the drivers seemed to be amused enough by us to guide us to the next appropriate bus.

The buses were an experience in themselves. Each one was absolutely crammed full of Thai people sitting, standing and crouched in the aisles so that each time we stopped practically everyone standing had to get off to let anyone at the back disembark. The rules for driving seemed to be to drive as fast as possible, to sound the horn as frequently as possible and to overtake anything at any point, whether safe or not.

The part I dreaded most though was the impromptu street sellers. It seemed that at any significant stop some little Thai woman may get on the bus and start to weave her way up the aisle selling packets of 'delicacies' for the journey. Needless to say, the Thai travelling delicacies aren't Werther's Originals or pear drops, but to my horror, packets of deep fried fish balls, locusts and worst of all, tarantulas. Dead or alive, deep fried or not, a spider is a spider and every time one of them would try and pick her way along the bus thrusting packets at people I held my breath, praying she wouldn't make it as far as our seats.

Somewhere along the seemingly endless journey, we picked up more backpackers and had our evening meal at a street café. Most of the menus in the larger towns and cities are in English and Thai, but every now and again at the smaller places we had to take pot luck, ordering several things from the menu and hoping we might like what we were served. Most of the time, the food was absolutely delicious.

I have no idea how we made it, but eventually, proud, amazed and tired we arrived in the border town of Aranyaprathet.

Wat?

Our first lesson about the Cambodians was that they have absolutely no sense of timekeeping. We sorted our visas out the night we arrived and were told to be up and ready for a 9.00 am pick-up to the border the following morning. So at nine o'clock sharp we were ready in the reception area of the hotel and waiting eagerly for our driver. At about 9.30 am we were told we had time to grab some breakfast and started to doubt the reliability of our collection.

Still, it gave us the opportunity to experience real Thai food with real Thai locals and we went in search of a café. After wisely selecting the place with the most customers, we ate a breakfast of Thai curry, pork with cashews and sticky rice washed down with a coke straight from the glass bottle – which for some reason always tastes so much better than from a coke can – and all for the bargain price of about fifty pence each.

Our 9.00 am pickup eventually arrived at around 11.30 am and we jumped in the minibus with a Scottish guy who we'd met while we waited. The border point of Cambodia was fabulous, with a mini statue of the temples of Angkor Wat forming an arch above the sign 'Kingdom of Cambodia' under which everyone has to pass. The roads were dusty red, it was baking hot and there were lots of people milling around, battered old cars beeping their horns and locals selling drinks from bikes, all creating a general mass confusion.

The second lesson we learned about the Cambodians is that they will lie when it comes to just about anything as long as they get your money. If we were told once to wait ten minutes for our next pickup the other side of the border, we were told twenty times. We waited over three hours. Fortunately, we were sat in a relatively comfortable, only slightly dusty, bar with a partially effective fan and plenty of cold beer. Plus, we had nowhere to be in a hurry.

We had expected our next ride to be an open-topped truck, but thankfully we were met by a somewhat battered, but enclosed car and a fourth fellow traveller in the form of 'Steve'. Steve's name is actually Mike, but for some reason, still unknown to any of us, Mike became 'Steve' and once it stuck, it stayed. He just looked like a 'Steve'.

I say the car was 'thankfully' enclosed, rather than an open truck, because the endless billows of red dirt on the un-surfaced roads meant that even inside, we were entirely covered from head to toe in a coating of dust once we'd been driving a few hours.

We drove through miles of red, dusty, potholed roads with almost no maintenance in a car with practically no suspension. As there are very few civilised towns en route to the city of Siem Reap, we stopped only for the odd comfort break, ironically usually quite uncomfortably in a bush at the side of the road or for a quick photo stop. It was amusing to see that when we did stop every now and again, small local children would appear from nowhere and giggle at us with nervous interest. I had my photo taken with a couple of really cute-looking kids who I gave a dollar note to and then promptly regretted having nothing else to give them as I wondered what use they'd have for cash.

When we arrived in Siem Reap, it was like discovering an oasis in the middle of a desert. Suddenly the potholed, bone-rattling, dusty roads became concrete and the deserted countryside led to bright lights and civilisation. Unfortunately though, our driver didn't lead us to the civilisation we wanted to be led to. It seemed that like the Thais, the Cambodians also worked heavily on commission and try as we might to direct our driver to our chosen hotel, he had other ideas.

We pulled up at the other side of town outside a hotel we didn't want to be at and were instantly greeted by several smiling men, eager to get us out of the car. However, holding onto our bags, we politely declined their offer of rooms and asked to be taken to the hotel we wanted and remained inside the car.

There we learned our third lesson about the Cambodians. If they don't get a successful sale, they can sometimes turn quite aggressive. The smiling men stopped smiling and started to shout and physically try to coax us out of the car telling us the guesthouse we wanted was closed. They really didn't want us to go elsewhere and at the point they made the taxi driver get out of the car, we started to get a little concerned. But we stood our ground and told the driver he wouldn't get paid unless he took us where we wanted to go. Eventually, thankfully we won the battle of the wills and the driver got back in and drove us away, albeit a little shaken.

Siem Reap is Cambodia's most touristy town and also the gateway to Angkor, the Kingdom of temples. Angkor was built over several centuries by ruling kings as a method of asserting their divinity, providing mausoleums and places of worship. The best known monuments are the vast temple of Angkor Wat ('Wat', meaning temple) and the walled city of Angkor Thom. Angkor also provided the film set for some of the action scenes in *Lara Croft: Tomb Raider*, although unfortunately that's the extent of my common ground with Angelina Jolie.

I'm not normally a churchy kind of person. Other than the obligatory visits to Westminster Abbey with the Guides and the usual weddings and christenings, I wouldn't ordinarily choose to spend much time visiting places of worship. But, I had it on good authority that Angkor was absolutely not to be missed and I must spend the full seven days there, the longest a pass would allow. I opted for a three-day pass to be on the safe side.

We hired Cambodia's version of a tuk-tuk and Emma, Steve and I headed out to Angkor to see what all the fuss was about. It's hard to describe what the experience of Angkor is truly like because you can't hide from the fact that there are thousands of tourists there and almost as many cheeky Cambodian children trying to sell you postcards or refreshments. The area is vast and very open and there is very little shade, save for the trees dotted about the place or the temples themselves.

You can walk around the site if you chose to, but to cover any real ground it helps to have a tuk-tuk handy. Our man stayed with us all day, following us round where we wanted to walk and picking us up for the longer journeys and all for the grand price of US$8 for the entire day.

There are so many temples to see and so much ground to cover that we picked which main ones we wanted to visit and spent our time leisurely going between them and making the most of our time, rather than rushing around like crazy. The whole place is absolutely amazing and even if you're not a temple person, it is well worth a visit for the sheer scale and rugged beauty of it. It really does give you a feel for Cambodia's history.

However, if you intend to climb the temples and really explore, then you need to have a basic level of fitness and a relatively good head for heights. The fitness wasn't a problem and I had absolutely no idea that height would be either, until I was about halfway up the steps of Angkor Wat. I didn't quite realise how very steep the stone steps leading to the highest point of the main temple were until I couldn't move my arms or legs through fear. There are no handrails and nothing to cling on to, while people just rush past you in either direction, plenty of whom I'm embarrassed to say were under the age of ten.

It was the first time I've ever experienced real vertigo and I only managed to make it to the top with the assistance of Emma who had to help me so as not to end up with us both stranded halfway up a temple.

The view from the top was amazing and we spent as long up there enjoying it as we possibly could to try and put off the inevitable climb down. To be honest, I would quite happily have contemplated staying there permanently if Steve hadn't come to our rescue and taken our bags and cameras so we had both hands free to inch down slowly – and I mean slowly. It must have taken us a good ten minutes to ease down, step by step like two-year-olds on our backsides, providing amusing entertainment for the hoards of people who seem to gather at the base for the sheer entertainment value of someone possibly slipping. Then as if the humiliation of public fear wasn't enough, when we eventually made it to the bottom, they all started to clap and cheer.

The other must do at Angkor is sunset – a very spiritual, moving experience watching mother nature change the colours of the day over one of the most sacred grounds in Cambodia. Or in reality, fighting your way up a steep slope to battle for a square foot of clear ground, among crowds of people clinging to piles of rubble, all fighting to get a glimpse of the setting sun, which if you're vertically challenged, you can barely see above other people's heads.

Crocodiles and karaoke

Cambodia itself, even in the more commercialised towns, is still very underdeveloped and tourism is relatively new, similar to how I imagine Thailand would have been about ten to twenty years ago. The people are so poor and desperate for money that they haven't quite grasped the concept of being overly hospitable to encourage tourists, which means they get quite frustrated if you don't buy something in their shop or chose their particular tuk-tuk.

Accommodation is plentiful and the restaurants serve wonderful local cuisine, which is similar to Thai food, if a little more basic. They also have a very relaxed, humorous attitude and there is a feeling of living for the moment in Cambodia. One of the funniest things about the country was the motor bike culture and how many wonderfully bizarre sights we saw on two wheels.

It became a bit of a competition to see who could spot the weirdest cargo or the most people on one bike. I remember seeing one man steering with one hand while reaching behind and supporting a ten-foot sheet of what looked like glass, wavering above his head. There were several bikes with numerous baskets of chickens hanging over the sides and on another moving bike, we counted a total of no less than six people, including three children and a babe in arms. Although the most peculiar sight without a doubt had to be a man with three pillion pigs.

The nightlife for tourists mainly consists of bars and restaurants and the Dead Fish Tower café in Siem Reap has to go down as one of my favourite bars in Southeast Asia. We stumbled upon the place by chance in a quest to try a new place each night and on seeing a sign on the entrance, which showed directions for the bar, rooms, toilet and crocodiles, we didn't really give it much thought.

However, not only was the bar one of the most attractive in the town, with wooden floors and tables and coloured scatter cushions on the raised seating areas, but it served great food, decent alcohol and the bar staff were friendly and welcoming. So we stayed all night, chatting and drinking, meeting other backpackers and befriending the waiter. It wasn't until I got up to go to the toilet that I saw the small bridge across a sunken pit, which was home to twenty or more baby crocodiles and rather alarmingly no safety measures in place other than a sign, which read, 'Crocodiles may snap'. Visits to the toilets then became far less frequent than they ordinarily might, after realising they were across the bridge.

That particular night was one of the best of the whole trip looking back, as it turned into one of those unexpected, spontaneous nights where you end up going with the flow and having a fantastic time. The waiter we'd been talking to most of the night was celebrating his birthday and invited four of us to go with him to a local club after work. So after plenty of sociable cocktails consisting of some unknown but very pleasant mixture, we all walked to the oddest club I have ever been to in my life.

At first it seemed fairly normal, with an outside bar area, tree lights and plenty of atmosphere and thumping dance music coming from the packed club inside. We were clearly the only white people there and the attention we attracted was quite unnerving at first, with our friend even having to persuade the management to let us stay. But once we were settled with drinks and the staring subsided a little, we had the most strangely fantastic night.

For a start, all the attention we were getting came from the women and was predominantly aimed at Emma and me. It was really comical, but the women couldn't take their eyes off us. I can only think it was partly because of the fact we were white and in their club and partly due to the fact that we were plastered and dancing like things possessed. So there we were, throwing shapes around the floor and on the stage of this hot little club, the room was packed and Emma and I had our own little dance troop mimicking our every move.

Suddenly the music stopped and before we had a chance to wonder what was happening, the lights came on, the floor emptied and a large white screen descended from the ceiling. I don't know whether we were more amused by the fact that a Peter Andre look-alike emerged from the crowd and started singing Cambodian love songs to a soft focus karaoke video, or the fact that no one batted an eyelid at how seriously he took it. Either way after several ballads and another round of drinks, 'Peter Andre' and his screen disappeared, the lights dimmed and the thumping music returned as everyone flooded back on to the dance floor until the next random session of crooning.

We left the club not too long before sunrise having befriended half the female population of Siem Reap and content in our delusion that we'd shown them white girls can dance.

The Killing Fields

The morning we left Siem Reap prompted another episode of bad luck, when we were late for the early morning pickup to leave the hotel and learned another valuable lesson of travelling. Always check, double check and recheck the room before you leave. I didn't realise I'd left my treasured and quite valuable diving watch on the bed when we checked out and no amount of pleading with staff over the phone would bring it back. But then in a country where they earn the equivalent of US$50 a month if they're lucky, an expensive diving watch is quite some find. Still, I wouldn't make that mistake again – or so you'd think.

That morning's drive to the Tonle Sap River took us through some of the most poverty-stricken areas I have ever seen with my own eyes. The roads were just dirt tracks and the houses were no more than pieces of corrugated iron sheeting held up by wooden struts or leaned up against other structures. There were kids barefoot and unclothed, dirty and wandering around, people with injuries and disabilities laying on the street and dogs and flies everywhere. It was a really disturbing and quite humbling sight.

That's the thing about Cambodia that differs from Thailand, the stark contrast in the development of the two neighbouring countries. Even though Thailand has some very deprived areas and some very poor levels of housing and lifestyle even in Bangkok, the tourist industry seems to exist away from that. In Cambodia deprivation is everywhere. Tourism is so young it is being built up among those conditions and because they are so much more apparent, provides an insight into the real Cambodia.

The boat we boarded to travel to the capital, Phnom Penh was absolutely packed full and our bags were loaded onto the only area left, the roof. There was already no seating left in the main cabin of the boat by the time we arrived, so we were stuck with the not so luxurious option of the crowded deck. We managed to find ourselves a space toward the front of the boat, wedged between the glass windows of the cabin and the token rail, which marked the edge of the deck.

I'm not the tallest of people and no one could ever say that my legs go on forever, but I started to wonder how comfortable having them bunched up under my chin would be in six hours' time. The answer turned out to be, not very. The first couple of hours were very cold and fortunately we benefited from being so huddled together and managed to make the most of the collective body warmth. But, as soon as the sun started to rise, it was quite obvious we had no shade, no sun-block and no chance of escaping without third-degree burns.

Needless to say that by the time we docked, we looked frazzled, tense and were desperately in need of after-sun. Phnom Penh was more deprived than Siem Reap by far and the beggars and street sellers will try anything to get money from tourists and passers-by. We even saw one guy decanting Fanta and Coke from large bottles and trying to put the lids back on the smaller glass ones to sell them as new and we promptly decided to buy cans from then on.

We spent a few days in Phnom Penh meeting up with an old friend of Emma's and learned that a lot of Europeans move to Cambodia because it's so cheap, so quite a few of the bars and cafes are owned by the English, Irish, German and so on. Our hotel room was only US$5 per night and when we saw the ceiling was falling in, the fan was almost ineffective and we had bedbugs, it became apparent why.

In addition to the temples of Angkor, I would say that there is one other visit absolutely not to be missed in Cambodia, but sadly for very different reasons. The Tuol Sleng Genocide Museum (Security Prison 21 [S-21]) is one of the most moving, emotive and tragic places I have ever been.

The Khmer Rouge, commanded by communist leader Pol Pot, was the supposed revolutionary force the Cambodians expected to bring peace and an end to the war in the mid-1970s. However, they did anything but and instead began a systematic process of communist re-engineering of the people, prompting international outrage.

S21 was a local school in Phnom Penh, seized by the Khmer Rouge during their reign of terror against the Cambodians and transformed into a primitive prison. The classrooms were divided into individual cells or housed rows of prisoners in shackles and the conditions and cruelty imposed were sickeningly inhumane.

Anybody suspected of anti-revolutionary behaviour was brought to the prison, often with his or her spouses or children. They were then subjected to horrific torture before being killed or taken to extermination camps outside the city, such as the notorious Choeung Ek, more commonly known as the Killing Fields. It is estimated that around twenty thousand victims were imprisoned in S21 in the four years it existed and to stare into their eyes in the rows upon rows of photographs, invokes an almost overwhelming sadness. However, it isn't until you read the scroll of chilling rules to the prisoners and see the instruments of torture and the subsequent bloodstains on the walls, that you get any idea of the scale of suffering endured by the Cambodian people.

Goooooooooood Morning, Vietnam

Feeling sombre after our time at S21 and the Killing Fields, we left Cambodia on a boat for a 'delta tour' along the Mekong River, headed for Vietnam. That was our last experience of the elaborate way the Cambodians manage to inventively stretch the truth. After two hours on a boat that actually had holes in and no air conditioning, a further four hours on a smaller, even more basic, boat and a bus transfer for the remaining six hours, we realised that was the end of our Mekong 'delta tour'.

It was on our 'tour' of the river that I realised I'd not learned from the loss of my watch and having failed to check, double check and recheck as we left Phnom Penh, I had left all the paintings and keepsakes we'd bought in Cambodia – in Cambodia. I couldn't believe I'd done it again, but having offered to carry the lot, this time I'd left Emma's things there too and we were gutted. The 'tour' guide who'd brought us through the border offered to try and find our things and bring them with the next group the following day, but given our experience of the Cambodians so far we didn't hold out much hope.

Our hostel in Chau Doc was on a hillside, which had fabulous views for sunset, and we decided to take out bikes and ride to the top. Until we realised how steep the hill was and our ride became an uphill push. I also started to feel the stirrings of what turned out to be a pretty nasty twenty-four hour bug and after having to stop and be sick behind a rock, spent my first twenty-four hours in Vietnam sweating out a fever and feeling like I'd been hit by a train. Still, the next day brought the shock arrival of our lost paintings and restored our faith in the Cambodian people.

I was so excited about visiting Ho Chi Minh City (previously Saigon) and was looking forward to the capital of the south more than any other in city in Vietnam. I had thought Bangkok was busy, but Ho Chi Minh is even crazier. The streets are wider and there are less street sellers, but the shops are larger and it seems that everyone, but everyone rides a motorbike. There is a song by Katie Melua with the line, 'Nine Million Bicycles in Beijing' and I wouldn't be surprised if there aren't nine million motorcycles in Ho Chi Minh. They are everywhere and when you look at a road junction there are so many of them you wonder how they actually manage to move, in every direction at once without hitting each other.

We had first-hand experience of the mêlée when we hired two scooters and their drivers to go to the Củ Chi tunnels. The tunnels were dug by the Viet Cong guerrillas in the 1940s to escape the Americans and are typically very small and narrow. They have since been widened for Westerners, but are still very dark, claustrophobic and a little unnerving.

Still, the tunnels weren't quite as unnerving as the journey to get to them and Emma and I soon slipped into giggles of nervous hysteria between breaths of exhaust fumes. As we sat precariously perched on the rear of our rundown old motorbikes, we could literally touch the shoulders of the people on the bikes either side of us and we were surrounded. Whenever we pulled away, I'd close my eyes and hold on with one hand and use the other to hold a scarf over my mouth to minimise the pollution. You couldn't help but think that if you managed to escape a brutal death under the mangled wreckage of a hundred bike pile up, you'd probably poison your arteries with the potent cocktail of exhaust fumes emitting from them.

The journey went on forever, or an hour and a half of dusty, bumpy discomfort, which felt like forever. The tunnels were a really interesting visit and amazing insight into the conditions the Vietnamese endured to escape the war. Most of them are too confined and unstable to enter, but there are sections you can crawl, or stoop your way through if you can bare the sense of claustrophobia. We also had a go at shooting, which can be done at the nearby range and drinking, which can be done from the street stalls, selling the novelty snake wine. I couldn't quite stomach the wine with the actual baby cobra inside, holding a scorpion in its mouth, but those who did partake assured me it was suitably disgusting.

Unfortunately our first night in Ho Chi Minh wasn't quite as pleasant an experience as we'd have liked, but as usual it was sort of my own fault. Having sat down at a street bar to have our evening meal we'd spotted a couple from the border crossing and decided to move across to join them. Having stood up and moved our chairs, I immediately realised I'd left my bag on the pavement and went back to get it. The whole 'check behind you as you leave' thing clearly wasn't sinking in with me and for the third time I managed to lose yet more belongings, as my bag had been stolen in seconds. Only this time it wasn't quite as easily laughed off because the bag not only contained treasured possessions, but also money, traveller's cheques, phone, camera, visas and both our passports.

The natural thing to do when you have something stolen is to report it to the police and see if there's any chance they may be able to help. So, with little hope of ever seeing my bag again, we decided to at least obtain a crime number for the insurance and headed off to the police station. I know the police in the UK come under constant criticism, but the Vietnamese really opened my eyes to bad practice considering we're in the twenty-first century. When we arrived at the rat-infested hole of a tiny station, the officer in charge barely even looked up from the television, let alone shifted his feet from the table he lounged against.

Fortunately someone spoke a little English and we managed to convey our situation to her, which she attempted to relay to the obnoxious officer. I don't know if he genuinely felt indifferent to our predicament or whether he was too ensconced in the TV to bother with us, but I could hardly believe it when our embarrassed interpreter translated his reply of, 'No one is interested today, come back Monday'.

Partly fuelled by annoyance at myself for having been so stupid in the first place and partly by my impulsive and stubborn side, I insisted we were going nowhere until we at least had a crime number and dragged Emma reluctantly inside.

It seemed that no amount of resolve could influence the ignorant officer to attend to us and the most attention we drew was to be ushered off of a decrepit table, as we tried to make ourselves comfortable after an hour's wait. We gave up in the end and left with the filthiest of looks and some suitable choice words directed towards the lazy excuse for a policeman, though thankfully in hindsight I don't think he heard them over the sound of the television.

Fortunately though, when we returned to the bar, one of the bar staff had supposedly apprehended the thief and managed to retrieve my bag and at least some of the contents. I was amazed to find my purse, although without the cash, all my traveller's cheques and unbelievably both our passports complete with the visas we needed to get into the other countries. I decided I could replace my phone easily and the loss of my camera would force me to finally go digital, so we'd actually had a lucky escape. Now if I could only learn to check, double check and recheck!

Heaven on Earth

After the chaos of Ho Chi Minh we travelled north to Mui Ne, which was a welcome haven of peace and quiet for the most part. The town is relatively small with only a scattering of hotels, bars and restaurants along the beach road before the centre where the locals live and work in the markets. It is definitely a place for relaxing, surfing and sunbathing. Although I'd recommend an early night if you want to get enough sleep because at 5.00 am sharp, a daily preaching and musical accompaniment is bizarrely broadcast over loudspeakers throughout town and even I couldn't sleep through that.

Having spent a day or two relaxing to make up for the stresses of our first few days in Vietnam, we decided to try our hand at riding a motorbike to the nearby, locally famed red dunes. We collected the keys and opted for one bike between the two of us, seeing as neither of us had more than a momentary wobble on a motor bike, once each on previous holidays. We got off to a questionable start, with me nearly creaming into a gate post and Emma, although admittedly far more controlled, being slow enough that we could have walked faster.

We decided the best way to learn was to just get on the road and before long Emma had it mastered and managed to get us to the sand dunes, remarkably without incident. However, we'd visited on the windiest day of the trip and if we put anything down on the sand for more than a few seconds to take a picture, we struggled to find it again. The dunes were very attractive, but the sandblast effect made for a short stay and I drove us tentatively back.

Having done my research I knew there was one place on the Vietnamese coast I didn't want to miss, so our next stop was my personal version of heaven on earth – the shopping paradise of Hoi An. Hoi An is a huge draw for tourists, but still manages to be really charming and quaint. Its centre consists of just three main streets, with plenty of smaller interesting side streets lined with souvenir shops, galleries, craft stalls and restaurants. But, the main attraction for the town by far is its rag trade.

All of the streets in Hoi An are packed with tailors and dressmakers with rolls of materials and reams of patterns, all competing to create personally fitted clothes at ridiculously cheap prices. Spending a few days trawling the tailors of Hoi An is the closest I've ever come to experiencing an addiction and how I imagine it must be for a compulsive gambler to try and exercise control in a casino.

You just can't help but get sucked in to the atmosphere and the temptation of 'just one more dress'. They measure you one day, take instruction on which design, material and colour you'd like and less than twenty-four hours later you can have a tailor made, beautiful suit, dress, skirt or anything you chose. And for those sceptics who may understandably question the quality of such hurriedly produced clothing, I can vouch for its longevity. Two suits, two dresses, one top and a skirt later I still wear my favourite suit to work weekly and dread the day it falls apart, from over wear, not from bad workmanship.

Hanoi and 'home'

When we eventually prised ourselves away from Hoi An, we continued north to Hue (and plenty of other towns beginning with 'H'). Hue turned out to be rather dull and uninspiring and having got ourselves lost in the centre we saw a lot more of the smelly, rundown and frankly a little dodgy-looking areas than we'd have liked to see. We took a boat trip down the ironically titled 'Perfume River', into which I think most of the city's sewage is dumped, with the intention of visiting a local and allegedly picturesque temple. Four hours later, courtesy of the Vietnamese's ability to match the Cambodians for truth stretching, we'd visited a temple under renovation, which we couldn't see for scaffolding, and had been chased out of a dirty lavatory by the angry attendant because we refused to pay for the privilege.

We decided not to spend any longer in Hue than necessary and booked onto the night bus bound for the country's capital city, Hanoi. The Asians aren't renowned for their driving and plenty a journey was spent holding our breath and closing our eyes as they overtook on blind bends or tried to play chicken with an oncoming truck. We even passed an overturned bus on one occasion, with dazed and bleeding people wandering aimlessly around the wreckage and yet our driver still didn't bat an eyelid.

The night journey to Hanoi, however, had to be the most frustrating of them all. I don't know whether it was necessarily a good thing, but in the dark we didn't have the fear of seeing what our driver was risking to take head on. We did have the irritation of having to endure the incessant interruption of his horn every ten or twenty seconds, which made the likelihood of getting even a wink of sleep nearly impossible. But, if there ever was a danger of anyone dozing off with exhaustion, it was quickly prevented by the relentless jolting from the uneven, potholed roads. Which, at worst caused everyone on the bus to be propelled from their seats and if you happened to be caught unaware then you'd end up somewhere between the foot well and the aisle.

Eventually, we arrived in Hanoi and were puzzled to be ushered from the bus into waiting taxis for the journey into the centre, but it became apparent that the streets of the Old Quarter can't accommodate buses. It also became obvious that like everyone in Southeast Asia, the Vietnamese also work on commission and it is almost impossible to get a straight answer from anyone who wants your business. After driving around the same central streets for ten minutes, pretending he didn't know the hotel we'd asked to be taken to, our driver insisted we get out and go to the hotel his friend owned. We refused to pay his inflated price for the drawn-out journey and when we tried to go to a different hotel, the staff seemed to be in cahoots with the driver and claimed they had no room.

We had little choice but to check into the hotel we'd been taken to and agreed a price with the manager for bed and breakfast with use of the internet facilities. We'd also collected a good deal of souvenirs and gifts from our travels so far and decided to take a walk into town to find a post office to send our things home and lighten our loads. Hanoi is a very cultural and attractive city, with a simple but cosmopolitan atmosphere and a very French colonial influence to its architecture. The main post office was huge and quite modern in comparison to the small, thrown together look of the street shops in the Old Quarter. We entered to find long stretches of counters with plenty of people, but none would apparently serve us. We were ushered from desk to desk before waiting for ten minutes at the international desk before the clerk informed us they were shutting and we'd have to come back tomorrow.

When things go wrong I tend to giggle quite inappropriately and Emma and I had become quite good at it, but at that point my patience was beginning to wear very thin. So, not impressed with having to lug our goods back to the hotel, we took the Vietnamese equivalent to a cyclo to save ourselves the effort. Cyclos are basically small, two-person seats drawn behind a man on a bike and are marketed at a rate of one US dollar an hour. We were in the carriage for no more than five minutes, for which we figured 5,000 Vietnamese Dong would be more than enough, being the equivalent of a third of a dollar and offered the payment.

It seemed though that the driver was expecting more and wouldn't accept our Vietnamese money and no amount of reasoning would convince him to accept less than a dollar. So I picked up my bags, put the local note in his shirt pocket and went to turn away feeling quite brave and in no mood to be reckoned with. Then something happened that left me quite literally gob smacked. The Vietnamese cyclo driver threw his head back and spat in my face.

I was so totally shocked and disgusted that for several seconds I just gawped at him like I'd lost the power of speech. I contemplated putting my bags down and telling him what I thought, but had no idea what I would do or say and almost instantaneously a crowd had started to gather. I was half afraid that if I put my bags down they'd be stolen or if I had a go back, I'd be arrested and thrown in some Vietnamese prison Bridget Jones-style. So Emma and I settled for swiftly walking away, sobbing with frustration and lack of sleep and shouting abuse at him as we went, just in case we hadn't lost enough dignity already.

It's such a shame that our first experiences in Vietnam had to be so unpleasant and that a few of the people there made such a bad impression. I really don't think all Vietnamese are that way inclined and I am sure it is mostly due to the fact that tourism is still relatively young, as it is in Cambodia. They are so desperate for money and for every opportunity to get it, that sometimes they resort to dirty tactics instead of realising that being polite, courteous and friendly would ultimately go much farther in the short and the long term.

However all that said, at that point my patience with the Vietnamese had run out and I couldn't wait to see the back of the place. It's a shame because we'd have gladly visited the coast and areas surrounding Hanoi, but all we wanted to do was to book a flight out of there and go back to Thailand, which by then felt like going home.

We had one night in Hanoi, which considering our experiences seemed a very attractive and lively place to be. But things didn't improve when fuelled by my now absolute contempt towards anyone who tried to rip us off, I argued the fee with our hotelier and he threw us out onto the streets with all our bags, six hours before we were due to go to the airport. Some people just never learn when to cut their losses.

Gin and ladyboys

As we landed in Bangkok we were tired, feeling a little low and tensions were running more than a little high. All we wanted to do was relax in the sunshine by a poolside, with a cold beer and get back our enthusiasm. I'm not quite sure which of the following discoveries tipped me over the edge that day, but it's fair to say I had a complete and utter sense of humour failure.

It may have been the fact that the pool in our high rise hotel turned out to be on the ground floor, surrounded on all sides by the building and therefore devoid of sunshine, or that when we checked our gifts and souvenirs, they had been broken by the rough airport baggage handlers. Either way, I remember feeling my anger reach boiling point, something snapped and I lost every last shred of rationale.

I grabbed the boxes of things to send home, barked at Emma that I'd had enough and suggested we go and get absolutely out of control drunk. I literally marched to the post office, not saying a word, feeling thoroughly fed up and festering in my own sulkiness. Once our things were packaged for posting, we headed straight for a little bar that we'd discovered before heading off for Cambodia.

It was a fabulously simple, tiny bar on the main Sukhumvit Road with a gay owner who was extremely camp, a ladyboy as the main hostess and the other waitresses were all prostitutes. They'd invited Emma and me in as we walked past one day and were so friendly and interested in us that we knew it was the only place we wanted to be. We walked straight in, ordered a gin and tonic and a bottle of beer each and stayed until they were clean out of gin.

We chatted to the women, watched with amusement as men came and left with different girls, or boys depending on their tastes and felt every shred of stress slide away. When we eventually left, it was dark and in a quest for more gin we wobbled our way along the road between the crowds and street stalls looking for another bar. That night didn't end with dancing or partying into the daylight hours, but it did end in fits of giggles in the Country Road.

Country Road being the next and last bar, complete with neon signs and the most bizarre long-haired, leather-clad Thai band singing old-style country music, which went something like this, 'Country load, take me home to the place where I berong...'

We spent a few days in Bangkok and met up again with Steve (from Cambodia). We visited Thailand's most holy site, the Grand Palace, which was magnificently opulent with every square inch adorned with jewels and gold. Although it's hard not to be impressed by the temples and stately buildings within the palace walls, it is difficult to approve of such a concentration of wealth, when so many people live in dire poverty on the streets outside.

Another compromise of values was the attire, so strictly adhered to in the Palace grounds. It is forbidden to expose shoulders or ankles and shoes must be closed, completely covering the foot. I'd heard about the restrictions, but figured that as long as you paid your entry fee, they surely wouldn't turn you away just because of a little exposed flesh. But it transpired that I couldn't have been more wrong and was forced into hiring the more 'appropriate' clothing they dish out at the entrance. I use the term 'appropriate' lightly because while it does cover any offending areas, I'm also sure they select each item for its bad taste value.

So, to my horror I reluctantly put on a pair of orange Velcro sandals, an old tattered shirt I hoped had been washed and a pair of blue socks that I refused to even contemplate where they'd been. I felt like a model for the Red Cross fashion show and hoped this wouldn't be one of those uncanny times when you run into someone you know, in some random place on the other side of the world.

That night we took Steve to the bars on the street where our hotel was and explored the infamous pole dancing clubs and strip joints of the Nana Plaza. It might sound odd for two girls to be trawling such seemingly male-orientated establishments, but as I previously explained, we only entered those where the girls encouraged us to and besides, we wanted to see what all the fuss was about.

I think Emma and I were considerably more comfortable than Steve once the buxom and rather large Madame (who was actually a Master) took a fancy to him. In fact, it was far more entertaining watching Steve squirm, while the Thai version of a pantomime dame intimidated him with her attempts to flirt than it was watching the girls perform inside. They looked bored silly and although they were stunning, their half-hearted efforts at dancing were only token moves between a lot of standing about and trying to catch the eyes of any men in the audience who might be up for a bit more than a lap dance.

We stayed for one drink, trying to guess which ones were genuine women and which had a little more to them than met the eye. Before we knew it, the girls were trying to drag Emma and me up on stage. It wasn't a packed venue by far and if I'm honest, other than us there may only have been a handful of other people there. But one thing I absolutely never, ever do is get up on stage and perform. I don't even do karaoke and I certainly don't take my clothes off in public (unless there's a creek and a stranger with a camera obviously).

Fortunately though, it was one of those rare moments on a drunken night out where the spirit didn't get the better of me and we managed to make good our escape. Much to his amusement, Steve definitely had the last laugh.

Stupid English

Emma's brother joined us in Bangkok, before we all flew down to the southern peninsula for Christmas on the islands. We had a rough plan to spend a few days on the tiny eastern island of Ko Tao, go to nearby Ko Pha Ngan for the renowned full moon party on Boxing Day and then move on to the West coast to visit Phi Phi before heading back to Bangkok.

Ko Tao, the smallest island on the east coast, is known for some of the best beaches and the best diving in Thailand and conjured up images of an idyllic paradise. The only way to get there is by boat and if we'd learned one thing about travelling in Asia so far, it was that nothing is straightforward. So, when we boarded what looked more like a cargo boat than an overnight ferry, it's because that's exactly what it was.

The lower deck had no glass in the windows, but then with the stifling heat it was probably a good thing. The floor was arranged with individual, very thin and threadbare mattresses without space between them, in two lines along either side of the deck. We learned that one side was for white people and the other for Thai people and that was to be our sleeping quarters for the entire twelve-hour journey.

When I imagined myself travelling around Asia, I had visions of being on dusty roads, in trucks full of sweaty bodies with random chickens clucking on their way to markets and all the other typical and seemingly authentic images you see on television. So, as I sat on my dirty mattress, surrounded by sweaty bodies and watched little Thai men load bags, bikes and crates of live pigs onto the boat, I smiled to myself and realised it was exactly how I hoped it would be.

About four hours later I was hot, tired and sick of the noise of grunting pigs, not to mention other random grunts coming from various orifices around me. It appeared that even the novelty of authenticity can wear off after a while.

We docked well after sunrise and the island didn't disappoint. The beaches were perhaps a little smaller than I'd expected and the accommodation a little closer together, but once we found our bungalows at the end of a beautiful white sandy cove, we were more than happy.

The resorts aren't huge sprawling family complexes with cabaret bars and hideous pools full of screaming children and water flumes. They are small arrangements of private bungalows, usually with trees and flowers separating them and a rustic bar or restaurant for the use of the guests. Ours was on the very edge of the beach with the water a stone's throw away and the first thing we did when we arrived was to swim.

You can't help but relax on Ko Tao, because there really isn't much else to do during the day but sunbathe, swim, dive or shop. Even if you walk or cycle around the island, there's not that much of it to explore, so you'd think you couldn't really come to any great harm there either. But Emma's and my capacity to attract misfortune seemingly knew no bounds and it wasn't long before a whole new disaster had befallen us.

On the day before Christmas Eve, we decided to hire a motorbike to explore the island and with our new-found confidence in our riding abilities, we were invincible. Our first stop was to a dive shop to book some trips for the next few days and then we travelled uneventfully to the other side of the island. We'd heard about a German chef who owned a restaurant and was taking bookings for traditional Christmas dinners and we didn't want to miss out.

So after a leisurely lunch to sample the food, we made our reservations and got back on our bike for the return journey. The restaurant was through a small clearing, on the edge of the beach and down a steep slope from the main road. Emma and I were sharing a bike and as she had driven to the restaurant, I was going to drive back. I felt quite confident because unlike the manual one we'd driven in Vietnam, these were automatic so they were bound to be easier.

We decided I'd reverse the bike before Emma got on and I very carefully pulled it backwards. I had been on the bike for no more than ten seconds, when I revved a little too hard and the bike shot forward a little faster than I had expected. Actually, it was a lot faster than I expected and I overshot the turning, panicked, pulled the accelerator instead of the brake and headed even faster towards a five-foot gatepost.

I was completely out of control, but I had one of those sickeningly odd moments of clarity, when it's as if everything has suddenly stood still and in a split second you manage to go through a totally rational thought process in your head. Right before I smashed face first into the gatepost.

I remember thinking that there was absolutely nothing I could do because I was going too fast and I was too close to the post to stop myself crashing. All I could think was that if the bike landed on top of me and I broke my leg, I'd have to go home, the trip would be over and I hadn't even been diving yet. So I decided in that split second to try and push the bike one way, throw myself the other to try and avoid the bike landing on me.

I realise this all sounds very dramatic and fanciful and I am in no way trying to create the illusion that I fancy myself as a stunt woman, or that I was in any way courageous or daring. I wasn't – it hurt and I have the world's weakest stomach when it comes to blood or maimed bodies, especially my own. But, the way the mind works when you're in the throes of disaster is amazing and I really didn't want to miss out on my travelling.

So, as I hit the post with my face, bit through my top lip, made my nose bleed and took off into the air while still sitting on the bike, I did my best Evel Knievel impression and fortunately when I woke up on the floor, the bike wasn't on top of me.

It wasn't one of my favourite memories of the holiday, or one of my proudest moments, as one look at my gashed leg and the feel of the hole in my lip and it was all I could do not to pass out again.

Still, there's nothing like a good drama and as if I hadn't caused enough of a scene I sobbed like a baby, half in pain and half as my worries of ruining my chances of diving or making it to New Zealand played on my mind. I'm worse with blood and injuries if I think about them and for the whole journey to the clinic that's all I kept doing, with particular attention to the fact I'd injured the same leg in the same place as in my accident in Greenland. So by the time we arrived, I'd worked myself up into an unsightly mess and felt thoroughly sick.

Thankfully I've never had to go to hospital in my life, other than when my dad accidentally pulled my arm out of its socket when I was two, but fortunately my memory doesn't stretch back that far. I had, however, heard plenty of horror stories about foreign hospitals and people coming out in worse conditions than they went in with and I was in no frame of mind for rational thinking.

It didn't help matters when as I lay on one of two narrow stretcher beds, in a very small and basic clinic at the side of a dusty road on the smallest island in Thailand, I smelled the distinct aroma of frying garlic. I realised at that point that the Thai medics were next door paying more attention to their lunch than they were to my increasingly painful leg and I started to freak out.

Emma was next to me and the two nurses, who clearly weren't accustomed to such shameless displays of adult emotion, appeared and babbled at me in incomprehensible Thai, until I heard the only word I understood 'suture'. With that I sat bolt upright and was about to make good my escape when Emma sideswiped me back onto the bed with her arm and the three of them pointed out that I could continue making a scene until the wound got infected, or act my age and have stitches.

So twelve stitches, several painkillers, two crutches and a bruised ego later I left the clinic and felt utterly sorry for myself. It was two days before Christmas, I couldn't drink alcohol because of the antibiotics, I couldn't dive in case of infection and I couldn't leave the island because I had to go back a week later and have the stitches taken out.

Still, on a positive note, once the drama was over and the ridiculousness of our run of bad luck dawned on us, we started to see the funny side and before long we were giggling so hard I had to be careful I didn't tear my lip open again.

It wasn't until I went back to have my stitches taken out (with one of the nurses doing her ironing on the bed next to mine) that I saw several other British people being treated for various exhaust burns, scrapes or other biking injuries. In fact, it is so common to see us hobbling about with bandages and plasters from various motorbike accidents that when I commented on it to the nurse in an attempt to make light hearted conversation, her simple response was, 'Stupid English!' and to be fair, there's not much you can say to that really.

Tsunami – Boxing Day 2004

For most of my life growing up, the thought of being anywhere but at home for Christmas horrified me. I couldn't imagine not waking up with my family, in the cold miserable weather, going through the same old annual traditions. Then when I decided to have Christmas 2004 in Thailand, I realised it was actually really good fun to break with routine and do something totally different.

Admittedly, our Christmas morning plan of snorkelling and swimming had to be modified after my little accident, but we did manage to find a tiny tree to decorate and Santa hats to get us in the festive spirit. We had our Christmas dinner at the German restaurant and opened the presents we'd brought with us and it was quite novel to have sunshine and sand on Christmas day.

When we went to the restaurant for breakfast on the morning of Boxing Day, nothing seemed different on Ko Tao. It was the beginning of another hot day, not a cloud in the sky, the sea was clear and still and everything was as it should be. We noticed that the restaurant staff was gathered around the television and some were trying to explain to other guests that there had been some sort of flood on the west coast, but we didn't really pay much attention.

In fact, for most people on our island, the day passed as any other and we shopped, lay in the sun and made plans for the full moon party that night. The only indication we had that something significant had happened was by word of mouth from fellow travellers and the constant coverage on the televisions in shops or restaurants. But the news was in Thai, which we didn't understand and the enormity of the devastation on the west coast hadn't properly filtered through.

We realised as the day progressed that an earthquake in Indonesia had created a tsunami which had hit the west coast of Thailand and the surrounding areas and that the destruction was actually far more serious than we'd first assumed. We still had no real comprehension of the scale of the catastrophe and Emma set off by boat to the neighbouring island for the full moon party. I had decided it would be foolish for me to go in my condition and to even try it with my luck would undoubtedly be tempting fate, so I stayed behind.

It was that evening at about 10.00 pm local time, (3.00 pm UK time), 14 hours after the Tsunami had hit the west coast of Thailand and six hours after my parents had resigned themselves to prepare for the worst that I decided to call home.

When I'm away I don't make any arrangements to call my parents regularly, I never call my friends or other family and they don't expect it. I always keep in touch by email and phone when I feel the need and that is how it works. We are a very close family, but my parents are not unreasonably emotional and certainly not unnecessarily excitable.

I will never forget the feeling when I heard the overwhelming emotion of my mum's voice breaking into floods of tears. Even my dad, ever rational, sounded indescribably relieved and I heard him start to tap away on his keyboard as he immediately began emailing everyone who had dared to enquire whether they'd heard from us. It was only then I began to realise the scale of what had happened.

I assured my parents that we were all okay and tried to explain how normal life was where we were and how unaffected Ko Tao was. I didn't tell them Emma was on a boat and I didn't tell them I was on crutches. I figured they had enough to deal with. It wasn't the time to dwell on what they'd thought had happened and we spent most of the conversation with me promising I wouldn't dive, swim or do anything else that involved getting in the water for a few days. Little did they know that ironically I couldn't, even if I wanted to!

As our island was on the east coast, it was protected from the tsunami by the mainland of Thailand and bordering Malaysia, so we had been oblivious to the wave, which hit the west coast at around 8.00 am local time. Dive boats were running as usual, the weather was fine and with no English-speaking coverage, conversation about the disaster was limited to minimal information.

I had friends who were honeymooning on the western island of Koh Lanta and were supposed to be coming to Ko Tao, so it was a huge relief when they arrived safely. We celebrated New Year's Eve on the beach, with what would ordinarily have been a fantastic atmosphere and a fabulous all-night party, but the mood was notably sombre.

We had planned to leave the island to return to Bangkok on 1 January 2005, but we had no idea whether boats would be running or what the conditions would be like offshore, so everything was very unpredictable. In the emails I'd been receiving friends were urging us to get off the islands for fear of any repercussions of the initial earthquake. We were only too glad to discover that our boat, a catamaran, was the only boat deemed capable of leaving the island.

Although the waters around our island were relatively calm, we soon realised that out to sea, it was a very different story. The catamaran had a lower enclosed deck, where the bulk of the passengers sat and the luggage was piled up at the front. On the upper deck, there was another enclosed area toward the front and an exposed area of seating toward the rear, where we figured it would be the most stable.

The journey was scheduled to be three and a half hours long and within fifteen minutes I was feeling a sense of dreadful fear. For all my mock dramatisation of the things that had happened to Emma and me so far, I wouldn't say I'm particularly dramatic in more serious situations, but for one of the few times in my life I felt genuinely scared.

As we looked over the edge of the boat to the expanse of water all around, it was exactly how I imagine when people describe the sea as inky black. The waves were huge and the water seemed to be rolling as one whole mass, rather than waves moving on its surface. As time went on, the troughs became so deep that we could look down into them as we were lifted on the swell and it felt as if the boat would tip right over and be sucked down.

The waves became so huge that they were crashing over the top of the boat and several times people's belongings were washed down the deck so we had to make a mad dash to grab things as they flew past. We were absolutely drenched to the skin, we had white knuckles from holding on so tight and people were being sick everywhere. I forced myself to focus on the horizon and concentrate to stop myself being sick and to try and take my mind from the panic wanting to well up inside me. I kept wondering, how they could risk a journey in such dangerous conditions after so many thousands of people had already died.

Eventually and with a great sense of relief, we reached the mainland and went downstairs to collect our luggage. We couldn't believe the state of the lower deck. The whole floor was swimming in several inches of water, every life jacket had been deployed, there was sick everywhere and the luggage was drenched through. People looked traumatised and we soon discovered that one of the waves had hit the side of the boat with such force it had cracked a window, flooded the lower deck and set fire to the television.

The most astounding thing was that there were queues of people waiting for the return journey back to Ko Tao and it became apparent that they were still planning on meeting the schedule, with the same boat and another full load. Unbelievable!

In the days and weeks after we left the islands, we became more exposed to media coverage about the Tsunami and we learned more and more about what had happened and how incredibly lucky we'd been. The stories of different individuals and experiences of families that we read and heard about were heartbreaking and tragic and the impact of the devastation was inconceivable. It certainly put our misfortunes into perspective.

I don't think I will ever appreciate the magnitude of the anguish my family went through as they watched the news on the morning of 26 December 2004. They have since told me how they had a phone call from a friend at 11.00 am who told them to turn on the television and how they watched in horror as their minds tried to process what they were seeing.

It breaks my heart when I imagine what must have been going through their minds while they watched a map on the screen indicating those areas which had been wiped out by the tidal wave and the stark realisation when Ko Tao was included within that area. They had no way of knowing at that time that the information was inaccurate. I now know that as my dad went upstairs to check the internet while my mum and sister remained glued to the television, they were all individually trying to comprehend what the facts were telling them, that we must surely be dead.

I can only try and relate it to when I have watched the horrors of disasters reported on the news and how far removed it all seems when it's not happening to you or anyone you know. Then to imagine how devastating it must be to have the incomprehensible heartache of realising it affects someone you love. An estimated 230,000 people died on that fateful morning. Mercifully, we were amongst the lucky ones.

Jungle life

Our next few days were spent quietly in Bangkok before we took the night bus to the northern territory of Chiang Mai, near the Burmese border. Chiang Mai is the centre for the treks to the jungle hill tribes and is a rustic, very charming town. Other than the few bars and cafes, the most worthy visit was the night bazaar. By far the largest we'd seen so far, it was full of handcrafted souvenirs, wooden carvings, jewellery, paintings and more, so like moths to a flame we were drawn in, as if we hadn't bought enough souvenirs already!

Our jungle trek was to last three days and two nights, the first night being with the Karen tribe and the second at an elephant reserve. I was really looking forward to getting down to basics, but one very real fear played constantly at the back of my mind and it had eight legs. I realise some people may think that someone with arachnophobia going camping in the jungle is pretty ridiculous and they'd probably be right, but I couldn't pass up the opportunity.

Fortunately I didn't encounter any actual spiders, but we did see plenty of evidence they were all around. As well as the webs hanging in some trees, we saw numerous holes in the ground the size of golf balls, each with the entrance covered in a sort of white, woven funnel shape, disappearing into the earth. It was enough to make me shudder, with the thought of the spider that could create a web of that scale and was more than enough to make me quicken my step.

The first day was all uphill, through thick jungle treading a narrow dirt track. Sometimes we had to traverse rivers on precariously slippery stepping stones and sometimes on crude bridges of bamboo trunks balanced across the water. In other parts, we were walking single file with dense trees on one side and a steep drop to the other, having to be careful not to lose our footing while staring at the beauty of the surrounding view.

The jungle was breathtakingly beautiful, with a bounty of vegetation riddled with streams, rivers and waterfalls. It was also scorching hot. Eventually, after a whole day trekking we saw the tribal village on a distant hillside. It crossed my mind that there was probably a reason they lived in such a remote location with such challenging access, yet tourists still managed to intrude.

The homes were wooden stilted structures of varying degrees of stability, largely constructed from bamboo. We passed women and men working, children playing and running around and pigs, chickens and dogs freely scurrying about between the huts and the odd battered truck.

We spent the evening in one of the larger huts being entertained by the families and children. The women cooked dinner on an open fire, the children danced and sang and the men did magic tricks while regularly hacking up their phlegmy guts. It was the sort of evening that just glides by in relaxed company, casual drinking and enjoying chatting and swapping stories with new people. There was no electricity, so the end of the evening was dictated by the last embers of the campfire and dim moonlight.

The following day we left the tribe with parting gifts of colouring pencils, pens and sweets for the children. We had a considerably less arduous journey for the first leg down the mountain as we followed the basic road providing the only vehicular access to the village. We soon diverted into dense jungle again and trekked some four hours before stopping for lunch and a swim in a beautiful pool with a waterfall as the backdrop.

The going downhill was quite tough on the joints and as ever, I suffered with a throbbing ache in my knee courtesy of my skiing disaster. But with such beautiful surroundings, I managed to take my mind off my knee and concentrate on the amazing colours. At times, we found the vibrant green jungle stretching away from us in all directions as we looked down on the treetops and cascading waterfalls, while at other times all we could see were the dense trees we walked through, the damp jungle floor and stunning pink and red flowers.

We came to rest that night at the edge of a river near the elephant reserve and thankfully our beds were somewhat more comfortable than they had been the previous night. The guides cooked our evening meal of red curry, pork, sticky rice and sweet and sour vegetables and we sat under the stars drinking Sang Som (Thai dark rum) until we fell asleep, exhausted.

The next day was scorching hot again and we had a real treat in store. The only place I'd ever seen elephants up close before was at the zoo and to see them effectively in the wild, was amazing. We were also given the opportunity to ride the elephants and jumped at the chance. You'd probably think that there are fewer animals that would be quite so sturdy and stable to sit on top of than an elephant and to be fair, that's exactly what we thought too. However, in reality, the small seat for two seems to balance precariously over the elephant's back and is secured by a single rope.

The elephant's back also moves considerably as it walks and as a result, the seat also moves, quite unnervingly. I'm not saying that I was scared in the same way as I'd been on the catamaran leaving Ko Tao, but my stomach definitely fluttered once or twice as our seat shifted with every step. The real nervous giggles set in as we approached the river and our creature stopped dead at the edge of the steep slope down to the water.

Clearly it decided the slope was too steep and unstable for its tremendous weight and would most definitely not have bothered getting wet if not for the persistent little Thai man forcing him to move on. With his hooked prodding iron, the man poked the elephant behind the ear until it quite literally squealed and reluctantly continued down the riverbank.

The huge feet tentatively picked out steps on rocks that looked too unstable to support them and Emma and I clung together with our eyes closed, stifling giggles and wondering how we'd explain any elephant-related injuries to our already harassed insurance companies.

We made the rest of the journey down river in a sedate version of white water rafting, mainly due to the lack of white water. When we arrived at the transport to take us back to Chiang Mai, I was absolutely shattered, thoroughly soaked through and aching like an eighty-year-old woman. We were exhausted and ready for bed, but I truly felt like the jungle trek had been one of the best experiences for me in Thailand.

Laos ... again

After our first failed attempt at crossing the border into Laos, we had at least arrived at the desired entry point for our second effort. We had another hair-raising drive to the border town, met some more great travel buddies and went to the official crossing to get our visas stamped.

I consider myself to be a reasonably intelligent person, but as I've already described, there are some occasions when travelling that you find yourself doing things you'd never dream of doing in normal daily life. So as our group stood, waiting at the border crossing in the early morning light, I didn't think twice about handing over my passport to the random Laotian woman who approached us out of nowhere asking for our passports, even though I'd never seen her before in my life.

It occurred to me as she hurried off with each of our passports and visas that not one of us had questioned where she was going, how long she would be or whether indeed she would come back at all. So, I got myself a cold drink, sat down and did the only thing to be done in such a situation, waited and hoped for the best.

Fortunately the woman did return laden with every passport, complete with the appropriate visa stamps and we finally made our way into Laos. We were to journey into Laos down the Mekong River on a slow boat for a total of eighteen hours. But, on seeing our boat for the first time, I shouldn't have been surprised to find it wasn't exactly a P&O ferry.

The queue at the docking area was already snaking its way along the road even before we arrived and the boats lined up on the river didn't look exactly robust. They were long, narrow wooden cargo boats with the main length enclosed in a box-like structure with glassless windows. As we filed on, the elevated rear end started to sink lower and lower into the water so that with every new person, bike, or piece of luggage, the water's surface rose alarmingly higher up the boat's side.

Thankfully, it finally dawned on someone in control of the boat's load that the laws of physics would ultimately prevail and, in short, we were sinking. The answer was to unload half of the people, luggage, bikes and random live animals onto an adjoining boat – through the windows. It was another of those comical moments when you compare the logic of the locals to procedures at home and marvel at the seemingly non-existent consideration to any form of health and safety.

With all passengers on board, the luggage loaded on the roof and the realisation we were crammed into a very compact space with only narrow wooden benches to sit on for nine hours at a time, we set off. There must have been close to a hundred people on board and as there were nowhere near a hundred seats, some were sat in the gangway, some in the engine room and some even on the roof. Oh and there was only one toilet.

The scenery was beautiful along the Mekong riverside – lush vegetation, sandy banks and the occasional small town with children running along the shore calling to us excitedly. We stayed overnight in a small transit town before travelling the final nine hours to the historic city of Luang Prabang.

When I eventually stood up from my wooden perch and hobbled my way on to dry land, I worried that full sensation might possibly never return to my seemingly numb and bruised backside. Ultimately though, I did regain feeling and smugly re-evaluated the merits of carrying a little extra flesh on one's rear for such unforeseen circumstances.

Luang Prabang is a small city, full of culture and history and the streets are lined with locals peddling their goods laid out on the floor. The markets were remarkable and very inexpensive and the people were the friendliest and most relaxed of all the Southeast Asians so far.

The level of development in Laos compared to the other countries we'd visited however was the most basic. Our accommodation and the general physical state of the town was very rudimentary. This was illustrated no better than when we settled down for the first night in our guest house and a rather sizeable rat scuttled from under the bed and disappeared out of sight into the wall. It was okay though because the following morning I noticed a woman selling barbequed ones on the street, so at least they were doing something positive about pest control.

The weather in Luang Prabang was the coldest we'd had so far and we spent our time wearing every available layer of remotely warm clothing we had. The town was also quite small so after visiting the night markets, we decided to take in a little culture and go to the 'ballet' being advertised at the local playhouse.

I have to say it was an odd experience right from the start, when the local women came through the audience and tied good luck charms to the wrists of all the women, while muttering some incomprehensible chant under their breath. So, before long we had grubby pieces of string attached to each of our wrists and with the run of bad luck we'd had, we were too scared to take them off in case some ancient Laotian curse befell us.

The production itself was very colourful and mildly entertaining, but the Laotians are so relaxed and do everything so incredibly slowly, that after an hour Emma and I were losing the will to live and had to make good our escape during the interval.

We left the following day on a bus journey which I feared could only end in certain death and against all odds, arrived safely in Vang Vieng. The town is essentially only a few streets in size and consists mainly of guest houses, pizzerias, bars and internet cafes. When we first arrived, we noticed that the eateries smelled of incense and were packed with groups of backpackers lazing around on raised seating areas and scatter cushions, while watching television.

We soon learned that the screens in most of the cafes and bars bizarrely played the television series *Friends* on a loop and that people seemed to be spending hours on end watching episode after episode and seemingly wasting entire days. The whole town had a laid-back student feel about it and before long the atmosphere started to rub off on us.

It didn't take long before we realised that the reason for the chilled-out ambience wasn't just the mindless brainwashing from too much television, but the alternative menu available quite openly. It seemed that each place had an ordinary menu of shakes, cakes, sandwiches and meals and a 'happy menu' of hash cakes, hash shakes and other delights blatantly advertised, with the respective prices for the extra special ingredient.

We fought temptation to give in to the lure of the happy cafes for several days and visited the nearby caves and lazed by the river, but ultimately resistance was futile. It started with a prolonged lunch, which stretched into several episodes of *Friends* and before long we were hooked. We also noticed other newcomers cast disapproving looks, as they in turn passed judgement on us for wasting precious time stuck in front of the TV, as we had judged those before us.

I remember looking around at all the bodies strewn across the café we were in at one point, people's eyes glazed over, staring blankly at the TV and it looked like the aftermath of some mass cult indoctrination. I realised at that point that we would have to break the cycle, or we'd be in danger of losing entire days and possibly weeks in that small, offbeat little town.

So, we dragged ourselves away one night and vowed that instead of going back the following morning, we would take a bus straight to the capital city and spend some time in Vientiane before we returned to Thailand.

Sawat-dii (goodbye) Southeast Asia

We didn't spend too much time in Vientiane as we wanted to get back to Thailand for a few last days there before we went on to New Zealand, but also because we were shattered and our enthusiasm for exploring the new and exciting, needed recharging. So, after a few hours wandering around the markets there, we hopped on a coach for the eighteen-hour journey back to Bangkok.

Fortunately this time our journey to Bangkok was continuous as we didn't have to change buses, so although it made the trip a little monotonous we could just relax and not worry about language barriers, getting lost or deep fried tarantulas.

We arrived on the Koh San Road at about 6.00 am to torrential rain and decided to stay in one of the cheaper, typical backpacker guest houses there for our remaining few days. I particularly wanted to visit the Bridge over the River Kwai at Kanchanaburi and because Emma wasn't fussed, I went with a local tour on my own.

The town of Kanchanaburi became a prisoner of war (POW) camp in 1942 and the base for construction work on the 415-kilometre Thailand Burma railway, which was to be a crucial link between Japan's newly acquired territories in Burma and Singapore. About 60,000 POWs and 240,000 conscripted Asian labourers worked on the line with little else than picks and shovels and under such treacherous conditions that it earned the nickname, the Death Railway.

An estimated 13,000 POWs and 100,000 Asian labourers, half of those Asians who began the engineering feat, were killed. Most of those who died are buried in Kanchanaburi's two war cemeteries, with the graves laid out in symmetrical lines amid immaculately kept lawns and they make for an emotive visit.

The railway itself is constructed of giant concrete pillars supporting plain steel arches and subsequently isn't especially striking. But when you consider the history, together with the beauty of its surroundings, it becomes quite awe-inspiring. However, while walking across the bridge itself it struck me as being a little too narrow for the hoards of people shoving past each other to get to the other side and back.

Plus, I didn't realise at the time that it is still very much in use and let out a little embarrassing yelp as the sound of the train's very loud horn sounded directly behind me. I turned to find the huge great train bearing down on me as it waited for the crowds to cram onto the alarmingly small waiting platforms dotted along the bridge's length. There is plenty to do in Kanchanaburi besides the bridge and we took a boat ride along the river, stopped for lunch, visited the cemeteries and war museum and then took the train to a nearby waterfall where we swam until it was time to leave.

Our final few days in Bangkok were spent making the most of the nightlife and I have to confess to feeling the overwhelming need for a pint of cider and some good old-fashioned home cooking. The food in Asia had been fantastic and Thai food is still one of my favourites to this day, with so many fresh and wonderful flavours. We'd tried snake wine, had curry for breakfast, seen things battered and skewered that we'd never before have even contemplated could be eaten, but what I wouldn't have done for fish and chips!

So, we asked around and found the prerequisite for every well-established cultural city worldwide – an Irish pub. O'Reilley's was like a little oasis for us that night and we sat down to sausage and mash, fish and chips and pints of cider and black and had prime seats next to the comical Indian, country-and-western-style, one-man band.

We were his number one fans and the only ones joining in and whooping with support at each of his karaoke-style performances. As the cider flowed, we shouted requests for 'Green Green Grass of Home' and 'Delilah' and before long were singing along, filling in the gaps of 'Who the fuck is Alice?'

We stayed far longer than we'd planned, so by the time we left to check out the night bazaar across town, we were feeling somewhat merry. Alcohol does not provide a good basis for shopping and I managed to waste the remainder of my Thai Baht on a pair of knock-off Bangkok Diesel trainers that were ultimately too small, but I bought them anyway because I liked the colour. Our final quest before we left Bangkok and Thailand for good was a visit to the notorious district of Patpong – home to the city's most prevalent sex industry. The district is full of bars, clubs, strippers and shows and it is all about making money from sex and is relatively expensive. We didn't bother with anything other than gin and good old-fashioned drinking, sitting in the street bars, meeting hoards of people and leaving it way too late, considering we had to be at the airport the following morning.

Emma's flight was the day before mine and we managed to successfully depart Thailand with as little drama as losing our airport tax tickets and having to buy them again after a mild panic. So, considering our catalogue of disasters including being turned away from the border at Laos, the numerous items we lost or had stolen, being spat on, a bike accident resulting in minor surgery, a tsunami and narrowly avoiding capsizing at sea, we considered that just to still be alive was more than enough to be thankful for.

I absolutely loved Southeast Asia and would highly recommend any of the countries to anyone. I'd perhaps not advocate that females should travel Vietnam or Cambodia alone and that even as two females together, you should expect a different treatment than you'd maybe get with a male companion. But, despite all the more challenging encounters, I loved every minute and they all play their part in building a colourful and fantastic overall experience.

As I sat in the airport waiting to board my flight to New Zealand, I actually couldn't believe that I was about to embark on another fantastic trip, after having such an amazing time in Asia. Every other time I'd been travelling it was to explore predominantly one country and then go home and I kept smiling to myself that I wasn't going home, but onto somewhere else.

I always intended to go back to Thailand and visit the west coast and to hopefully dive as I couldn't in 2004. I wanted to see the effect of the damage caused by the tsunami and to support the local tourism and obviously to visit a part of Thailand I hadn't already seen. I also loved the intoxicating vibrancy of Bangkok and knew it would be one of my favourite cities in the world.

So, as I write this paragraph, I am excited to say I have only three weeks left until I fly out to Thailand for the first time since my last visit. I am going to spend time on the island of Phi Phi, diving and swimming, (hopefully injury-free) and then I plan to spend three nights in Bangkok where one of my first stops will be a small bar on the Sukhumvit Road, where I hope they'll have restocked the gin.

Sally Wootton

The dolphin pod, Kaikora, South Island

New Zealand, Tamaki Maori
Village, North Island

Going Home, Christchurch,
South Island

The Wizard, Christchurch,
South Island

Michelle, Sally & Bobby! Dunedin, South Island

The Abel Tasman national park,

113

New Zealand 2005

One of the dusky dolphins showing off

Bobby and me canoeing in the Abel Tasman national park, South Island

Paradise. The Abel Tasman, South Island

The Queen Charlotte Walkway, South Island

Huka Falls, Taupo, North Island

Wai O Taopu, North Island

Cinema Paradiso, Wanaka

The Queen Charlotte Walkway, South Island

Wai O Taopu, North Island

115

New Zealand 2005

In my element! Franz Josef Glacier

Me on the Franz Josef Glacier - again!

The mouth of the Franz Josef Glacier, South Island

Exploring the Franz Josef Glacier

This one is on the cover! Franz Josef Glacier South Island

The Queen Charlotte Walkway,

Mi fabuloso hermana, Sonia. Pienso en usted menudo

Monserrate, Bogotá

Grenadilla or 'snot fruit'!

Platano squishing at the finca outside Bogotá

The making of THAT sweet, Moniquira

A day centre for disabled young people, Villa Vicencio

The 'tuna' at the Escuela de Cadetes de Policia, Bogotá

Me licking the walls of the Minas de Sal, Bogotá

117

Colombia 2008

Anne and me with mi familia en Colombia, Sonia, Ricardo, Mami y Paola

Addressing the conference at Paipa

The festivities in full swing at Paipa

Steve and the boys at the after party, Paipa

Raoul's rotary club at Villa de Leyva

Children at a local school, Ibague

118

Colombia 2008

The brave soldiers of VII Brigada who have sacrificed so much for their country

Us with the orphans of Ibague

'The Godfather' or 'Bugsy Malone'?! Sogomoso

Making guns at Sogomoso. We were a few feet away with no protective clothing!

Making friends with the local police! Bogotá

An official group photo at Sogomoso

Colombia 2008

Colombian 'Bobby'

Weapons seized from
the guerrillas by the VII
Brigada, Villa Vicencio

A poster showing the faces of those kidnapped by guerrillas, Ibague

The General gives his troops their final briefing before they leave to intercept the drug traffickers, VII Brigada

Diving

An ugly moray eel, Egypt

Typhoon, Red Sea, Egypt

Me on the toilet! Egypt

A Thai Turtle, off Phi Phi island 2009

Nemo!

The best group of holiday buddies ever, Red Sea, Egypt May 2007

Diving

Me looking good?! Red Sea Egypt

Great Barrier Reef, Australia 2003

In the Blue, Thailand 2009

Wally the Napoleon wrasse, Great Barrier Reef 2003

Me on the reef, Australia 2003

New Zealand 2005

The north of the North Island

On my arrival in New Zealand, I hooked up with Emma at the house she was sharing just outside Auckland and my next travel companion joined us a few days later. Bobby was one of my best friends from home, not a seasoned traveller and her one instruction to me was categorically not to even consider trying to get her to do anything that involved throwing herself from any great height.

We spent five days with Emma and her housemates living their party lifestyle and I discovered that somewhere since leaving university nearly ten years previously, my body had lost the ability to sustain round-the-clock partying. One big night a week is my limit at best, so we left with an emotional goodbye, or at least it would have been if I had been sober enough to appreciate it and Emma had been sober enough to remember it. Bobby and I went to catch our early morning bus with me in a state of severe hangover and Bobby shaking her head in despair as I repeatedly muttered the only words I could muster, 'Oh my god, oh my god, oh my god!'

Auckland is a fairly ordinary city as cities go, with a crude grid-like system of long sloping streets, interspersed with a few pretty parks and a developing quayside. The Sky Tower is the main structural attraction, although it is essentially a smaller version of the CN Tower in Canada. There are plenty of shops and cafes as one would expect, but shopping was disappointingly no cheaper than in the UK.

We also took a boat to the volcanic island of Rangitoto, which is the result of an eruption from New Zealand's youngest and largest volcano about 600 years ago. There's not much there, and although the walk to its relatively low summit was reasonably gentle and unenergetic, it was a scorching hot day and unsurprisingly, I managed to get burned.

Unfortunately though, the sun didn't last and we soon realised that New Zealand has a climate that for the most part is relatively comparable to the UK. In short, it rains a lot. It rained every day we were in the Bay of Islands in the North Island and our first night was spent in an NZ$80 per night guesthouse where we were kept awake by the all-night party going on in one of the adjoining rooms. All-night partying just isn't as fun when you're not directly involved.

We moved the following day to a more suitable guesthouse for the more 'mature' traveller and despite the bad weather, took a long walk to a supposedly nearby waterfall. I say supposedly, because after twelve kilometres in flip flops and steady rain it wasn't exactly the scenic stroll I'd envisaged.

Our last day in Paihia was wetter than all the others put together, but this time we paid for the privilege. The 'Excitor' promised to be a high-speed, enthralling boating experience consisting of a two-hour journey atop the crashing waves, culminating in a thrilling dash through an archway in the rock formation. In reality, we got sore backsides, were soaking wet through and had to turn back without any dashing through the rock, due to unsurprisingly bad weather, which made the conditions too dangerous.

Our next destination of Whangarei was somewhat more sedate a location and chosen due to it being the nearest town to the Poor Knights Island where I intended to dive while Bobby relaxed. The owner of the hostel we chose turned out to be a rather eccentric old man with an extraordinary talent for drawing. He exhibited his work locally and ran the hostel with his wife as a means of income. I couldn't help being completely overwhelmed with his drawings and after a particularly emotional evening following my day's diving, we sat and chatted and he convinced me I couldn't possibly continue through life without buying one of his pictures.

Not to be defeated by the miserable weather, we hired a couple of bikes (ones without engines I hasten to add) and cycled the 36-kilometre round trip to Hot Water Beach. The beach is promoted as a small secluded bay where you can allegedly dig holes in the sand and relax in the soothing hot water that bubbles up from the natural springs, while watching the waves gently lapping at the shore.

We arrived at the beach at around the same time as seventy-five other tourists and soon discovered that the thermals only exist in about five metres square of beach. So, if you managed to fight your way through the crowd to the precise area, you then had to force your foot deep enough into the sand to actually locate any hot water. You would then be promptly scalded as it really is that hot, but immediately cooled down as one of the frequent large waves crashed over the crowded beach, depositing numerous jellyfish as it receded. Not quite the idyllic paradise we were expecting I have to say.

Strange smells and strange folk

Our mode of transport for getting around New Zealand was the Magic Bus. That isn't to say we would step on board only to find ourselves mysteriously transported to each location Harry Potter-style. It was just the alternative to its rival company Kiwi Experience and recognised as catering for the more mature clientele.

We travelled through the pine forests and wildlife reserves of the Coromandel and then on towards the thermally heated town of Rotorua. However, before we arrived in the town, we took a slight detour to the Waitomo Caves. The caves can be explored in a number of ways and we chose to take inflatable tyres down to the deepest caves and float through them on the rivers that run through their base. We had to be properly kitted out with hard hats, torches and wet suits. When we reached the first cave, we put our tyre in the water, sat inside and floated down river in convoy.

When we reached Te Anaroa, the largest cave, we were told to switch our lights off and look up towards the ceiling. There, hanging from the roof of the cave, was a carpet of tiny blue lights, shimmering above and lighting up the ceiling like thousands of tiny fairy lights. The lights were coming from glow-worms each the size of matchsticks, which are apparently, for the science bit, the larvae of mosquito-like gnats. They were really breathtaking and odd to think that they are glowing so far beneath the ground.

We then got into our rings floating in the pitch black of the caves, staring up at the glow-worms and enjoying the relaxing pace and peaceful surroundings. Bobby told me later that she had been praying I wouldn't notice the numerous spindly spiders clinging to the cave walls, which thankfully I didn't. After our sedate and relaxing float downstream, we reached a waterfall and were told the alarmingly inventive method we'd be using to get down it. We had to get out of our rings and put them behind us as if we were about to sit down in them. Then we had to turn our backs to the waterfall, lean back and let gravity do its thing, while hoping that we'd land in the water, still sitting in the ring. Bearing in mind that we had no idea how high the drop was or what was at the bottom and all of this was in almost pitch blackness. Still, I figured that the guides knew what they were doing and that killing or seriously maiming customers was probably frowned upon, so we took the leap. It all sounds a little more dramatic than the reality if I'm honest and the drop was only about six feet, but I'd be lying if I said I didn't close my eyes and let out a little squeal.

Rotorua was probably one of my favourite places in New Zealand and it certainly had the most character, not to mention the most pungent aroma. The whole place is built on geothermal rock and the natural springs and minerals create a constant sulphurous air. In short, it absolutely stinks!

I found most of the towns in New Zealand eerily generic and lacking in character. There seems to be no distinction between the locals' way of life and tourism. The shops are all aimed at tourists, selling the same generic gifts and typical souvenirs, the guest houses are among residents' homes and most towns are on the whole very small and insular. But, in a country twice the size of the UK with a population of only four million and a huge tourist industry, I suppose that is hardly surprising.

One of the things I wanted to try in New Zealand was a traditional Maori feast called a hangi. They cook meat, fish and vegetables in clay ovens in the ground and it is absolutely delicious. So, we joined one of the organised tours and went to the Tamaki Maori village just outside Rotorua for the whole experience of a true Maori cultural evening.

On the bus journey to the village we had to select a 'chief' from one of the men in the group and somehow an Aussie bloke called Sid was nominated. Sid was a bespectacled, balding portly man in his latter years and sort of sacrificed to represent us 'white folk' in the evening's festivities. As we arrived at the village, we were met by a welcoming party of Maori tribesmen who pretty much scared the life out of us.

They are on the whole huge guys, they adorn themselves with war paint and run at you waving big sticks while bulging their eyes, grunting loudly and sticking their tongues out. What Sid didn't bargain for was having to join in and try and mimic their routine, while we all watched. The hardest part was trying not to laugh because it is actually a traditional and time-honoured performance and to laugh is apparently disrespectful.

The village was laid out as a typical Maori village would have been and the people were so passionate and proud of their heritage and culture. The dances and performances all depicted some different aspect of Maori life. If I'm honest I can't say I could see a great difference between the dance depicting a hunt, the war dance or any other dance, but whatever the performance there was always plenty of tongue waggling, eye bulging and belly slapping going on.

I really liked the Maoris and it was so apparent that as a country, New Zealand is hugely proud of its history and its culture. So when we returned to the town that night, we toasted their heritage right through to about 3.30 am.

The following day was spent rather more sedately and I would highly recommend not waking up with a hangover in a town that smells of rotten eggs. After browsing the shops for the same gifts and souvenirs we'd seen in every other town, we decided to check out the Polynesian Spa in the Government Gardens. With a juxtaposition of the prim and the exotic, the gardens give the impression of a typical English village with colonial influences and a few palm trees thrown in for good measure.

The spa itself is the sort of place you could happily go to and lose yourself just lazing and soaking in the hot pools until you shrivelled up like a little prune. The setting is simply idyllic with all of the open air pools looking out onto a clear blue lake, with white rocks and the hills framing the scene in the distance. That is, unless you're unfortunate enough to go at the same time as twenty or so Japanese tourists, who obviously have to all sit in the same pool at the same time and block your view while taking at least a hundred photographs.

Crowds aside, I loved the spa and it was certainly just the thing to ease an aching head. We spent our last night on the smoking terrace of the closest thing we could find to a real pub, not because either of us smoke, but because the smoking ban had been recently introduced and the inside of the bar was so deserted we initially thought they were closed.

Going down

We continued our journey down south towards the South Island and visited the Wai-O-Tapu thermal park, which was absolutely stunning. The area is built on volcanic rock and scattered with geothermal pools, bubbling mud and geysers. The colours are amazing and so beautiful that you can hardly believe that the greens and blues of the water are natural. The lakes and pools are bordered by white rocks and orange and yellow sand and the trees are the lushest green. Unfortunately, for us, we were on quite a tight schedule and I managed to fall out with the bus driver for insisting on exploring the farthest reaches of the park and getting back late. But it was well worth it and I would recommend a visit to anyone, but be aware that with geothermal activity comes that smell of rotten eggs.

We moved on to the town of Taupo with the main intention of using it as a base to do the Tongariro crossing, which is an arduous trek over the volcanic mountain and a famous challenge of the North Island. But unfortunately the weather took a turn for the worse and the most challenging trek we had was a flat walk along a beaten track to the crystal clear waters of the Huka Falls.

We waited for nearly a week, but alas the 80-kilometre winds and driving rain made the conditions too hazardous and the route was deemed too dangerous to pass. I didn't think being swept off the side of a mountain would have gone down too well with the insurance company after two thefts and a motorbike accident.

So, we left for Wellington and booked into the grottiest hotel we'd stayed in yet, with the squeakiest beds and promptly booked out a day later. Wellington was lovely, but its main attraction, other than shops and nightlife, is the Te Papa Museum. We'd had countless recommendations to visit the museum from people who claimed they'd been lost in there for three and four hours at a time. Museums aren't really my thing, but curious to see what the fuss was about Bobs and I hit the sixth floor and worked our way down. There were some interesting exhibitions and the science section was worthy of note, but the pretentiousness of some of the pieces was baffling. I decided they must have truly lost the plot when we saw two seemingly plastic apples, each on a white plinth, sectioned off with security ropes and titled 'Apples. Red and Green'. So, three quarters of an hour later we skipped the third floor, played with the 'change your own face' computer program in the kid's section and headed for the gift shop.

We left Wellington and caught the ferry to the South Island, which is absolutely beautiful and unbelievably diverse. Our first stop was Picton, which looks very much like a well-manicured English seaside town, except for the picturesque fjord harbour and mountain backdrop. A lot of people don't stay much longer in Picton than it takes to disembark the ferry and hop on a bus to the next town. But if you bother to take a little time, there is a very under promoted walk that can be done around the fjord edge with the most stunning views.

The Queen Charlotte Track winds through the mountain forests, overlooking the bright blue, sun-drenched fjord. If you have time you can take several days to walk the relatively easy-going seventy-one kilometres and stay at some of the quaint little B&Bs along the way. But, we decided to do just one day's worth of walking, covering fifteen kilometres and opted for a blueberry muffin stop instead. The views were absolutely breathtaking, but the easy-going route was made rather painful by the fact that it was here I discovered the knock-off Bangkok Diesel trainers I'd decided to wear were obviously a size too small.

We moved on from Picton to Nelson, which is the town that most people seem to head straight to after arriving on the South Island. We stayed in a charming little hostel, aptly named Shortbread Cottage after the home baked biscuits they are locally famed for and leave out as complimentary snacks for residents. The only trouble is, they're so delicious you find that after one you want another and another and another, then before long you're so hooked that you're almost obsessively contemplating ways of trying to sneak another fix and acting like some out of control shortbread addict.

We eventually managed to prise ourselves away from the biscuits and spend a day in the stunning landscape of the Abel Tasman National Park. The park is absolutely beautiful, with miles of white sandy beaches, crystal clear waters and lush green bush land. We didn't have a great deal of time in Nelson, but with hindsight I'd have gladly spent several days walking through the Abel Tasman to do it real justice.

However, our fleeting one-day visit started at 6.30 am and we made our way by shuttle to the kayak point. We met our guide and had a swift briefing on how to drive/steer/float the kayak, before setting off with more than a little trepidation. But, with me steering at the rear and Bobby navigating from the front, we spent a fabulously relaxing day calmly paddling on the turquoise water, soaking up the sun and generally feeling like we'd died and gone to heaven.

After our final day in Nelson catching up on emails and phoning home, we moved on and spent the day travelling through spectacular scenery. We passed through the deep blue green lake of Buller Gorge with its mountain backdrop and visited the impressive and unusual formations of the pancake rocks, which consist of layers and layers of limestone weathered away to look like piles of giant pancakes. So with the same overzealous camera action I displayed at Ayers Rock, I took a ridiculous number of photographs of what are essentially, yet again, just rocks.

As you journey through New Zealand, one thing that is startlingly obvious is the amazing fresh green and lushness of the vegetation and forests. The air is so extraordinarily clear and the lack of pollution is unbelievable in such a developed country. That is until you remind yourself that there are on average three sheep to every person in New Zealand and the equivalent of rush hour in most towns is the rare event of more than ten vehicles on the same stretch of road.

We arrived that evening in the town of Franz Josef, famed for being the gateway to the world's steepest commercial glacier. It's remarkable to think that we woke up in a town on the edge of white sandy beaches and turquoise waters and went to sleep a few hundred miles down the road at the mouth of a huge carving glacier.

Adrenalin overload

There isn't much to do in Franz Josef other than the glacier, but to be honest what else would anyone in their right minds want to do in such a beautiful landscape. So having decided to do the full-day glacier hike, I got myself ridiculously overexcited and persisted in boring Bobby with tales of Greenland and making too many comments along the lines of 'last time I was on a glacier...' etc. Yawn!

We started our day at 8.00 am and having been kitted out with hiking boots, crampons, hats, gloves and waterproofs, I was like a hyperactive kid on too many E-numbers and the distribution of ice axes nearly tipped me over.

The sight of the glacier when it first came into view was nothing short of incredible. Its body stretched down the valley to the snout, covered in debris while the rear disappeared into the mist of the clouds beyond. It took us forty-five minutes to walk from our truck stop to the edge, which looked far closer than it was in reality. Then, once we'd kitted up, we stepped onto the ice and I really felt like I was back on familiar territory.

It was weird actually to feel so at home doing something I've only really done once in my life, but I loved it. I also felt completely in awe all over again when I saw just how steep the ice wall was and how sharp and unforgiving the surface. I always imagine the moon to be like the surface of a glacier and find myself marvelling at the formations of the ice, from the tiny little clusters of crystals underfoot to the towering warped folds and tunnels as the surface ice has moved and buckled.

We spent all day traversing the surface, climbing over steep ice hills, down sheer faces and through arches, with bright blue walls of clean ice. There were several points where I felt reasonably unnerved and if I'm honest, quite frankly, a little scared. We weren't harnessed together and there seemed very few safety precautions and I couldn't help thinking of the power of such an unpredictable environment. Then I thought, 'Get a grip and stop being a drama queen, you're on a day trip with a tour company'. I needn't say how many photos I took on the glacier, but suffice to say Ayers Rock combined with the pancake rocks had nothing on the ice rock and I went to bed with a smile on my face. I woke up, however, without a smile on my face and walking like an old lady with the onset of rigor mortis.

I'm not sure at what point we decided on what we were about to do that day, but I do remember that at various points during the trip Bobby's point-blank refusal to do a sky dive had gradually mellowed and she decided that she'd give it a go if I did. I'd made up my mind I'd probably have a second go before we left the UK, but if I'm totally honest I think my nerves were increasing as Bobby's diminished.

Nonetheless, by the time we arrived in the town of Wanaka, we'd already booked our plane and by the time we arrived at the drop zone I was doing my best impression of someone who wasn't absolutely petrified. Having got up ridiculously early for the past two days, I hadn't bothered doing my hair or making much of an effort and having spent most of the previous day exposed to the elements, I resembled some sort of wild-haired, red-faced, half-crippled hag. Imagine my joy then, at meeting my young fit dive instructor who resembled a tanned, taut, rather easy on the eye catalogue model.

I mumbled some lame, embarrassed excuse for my haphazard appearance only to be even more horrified as a video camera was shoved in my face and the overenthusiastic camera bloke insisted I give a cheesy 'thumbs up' and tell all the folks at home, 'How I'm feeling right now'. 'Pretty damned scared and annoyed at the stupid camera man' would have been my grumpy reply.

Before long, my embarrassment for my hair was soon forgotten as they taped my sandals to my feet – flip flops are apparently not appropriate footwear for sky diving - placed a condom-like hat on my head and handed me a pair of conical-shaped goggles, not dissimilar to Madonna's pointy bra in the 'Vogue' video, but transparent and strapped to my face. As if it's not embarrassing enough to watch a replay of yourself dangling from someone's chest, with your cheeks flapping and rippling furiously, droplets of saliva flying from the corners of your mouth and all while you try not to look absolutely terrified.

However, despite all the embarrassment, my second sky dive was every bit as mind-blowing as the first. I think I even enjoyed it more, mainly because I knew what to expect and wasn't half-anticipating imminent death.

Our evening was considerably more sedate, if quirky, as we decided to go to the cinema, but with a difference. The Cinema Paradiso in Wanaka is a small locally run business, which specialises in warm cookies and a unique seating arrangement. All the chairs in the cinema are brought in from different places and consist of sofas, arm chairs, coach seats, folding seats and the most bizarre of all, an old, roofless Morris Minor.

I'm slightly ashamed to say that the novelty of watching a film while sitting in an old, bright yellow car inside a fully furnished cinema got the better of me and we were queuing up for more than an hour before opening time, just to make sure that absolutely no one got there before us. Then when the doors opened, we all but ran towards the Morris Minor. I'd like to think that if someone had tried to pip us to the post

I'd not have been so desperate as to resort to physical violence, but I wouldn't like to swear to it. And for the record, yes, the film was better simply because we were sitting in a car.

South of the South

Queensland is renowned as the 'crazy town of the South Island', full of adrenalin-filled sporting activities and supposedly the place to go for a wild time. However, whether we simply arrived at a quiet time, or just didn't make the most of it, for us it was by far one of the most uneventful places we visited. Admittedly, neither Bobs or I were interested in bungee jumping – me because I survived one about fifteen years before and vowed never to repeat the experience and Bobby because she'd exhausted throwing herself from a great height with the sky dive. We also passed on the white water rafting, jet boating, zip wiring, canyoning and everything else energetic and opted to save the last of our money for other things and chill out.

The most adventurous we got was to spend a very grey and wet day on the Milford Sound cruising the fjords and waterways, but even when we went out in the evening the town seemed quiet. We did manage to hook up with Michelle, an old university friend of mine who was also travelling and proved that it really is such a small world when you think about it.

Our final destination in New Zealand was Christchurch, but several stops along the way took in the wildlife of Dunedin, known as the 'Edinburgh of the South', the bizarre, perfectly spherical Moeraki Boulders and the stunning beauty of Lake Tekapo. The lake is even more deeply coloured than Canada's Lake Louise and with the distant backdrop of the snow-capped Mount Cook, it just takes your breath away.

Dolphins and wizards

When we arrived in Christchurch I have to admit to being quite relieved that we'd be staying in one place for a few days, until that was, we decided not to. The one thing left on my list of absolute must dos was to swim with dolphins and we'd heard by recommendation that one of the best places to go was Kaikoura, one hundred and eighty kilometres north of Christchurch.

But, we couldn't face another journey immediately, so we opted to spend some time wandering around the city and taking in what was to be our last destination of the trip. Christchurch is a very pretty city, with the main focus being its cathedral in the very centre. The streets are cobbled in places and the roads are wide and uncongested for the most part.

Our backpacker hostel was one of my least favourite, but at that stage the cheaper option, though I wouldn't recommend the chain of 'Base' hostels, unless you want to stay in huge, impersonal and very basic accommodation catering for the masses. But, then at the grand old age of thirty, I was about ten years older than the majority of its occupants and I won't feel guilty for wanting to go to bed at a reasonable hour, without being woken up at 3.00 am by drunken teenagers.

Besides, I think that while I'd enjoyed every second of my travels, the novelty of living out of a rucksack that I'd repacked more times than I'd changed my clothes was starting to wear off and my tolerance levels were beginning to wear thin by that point.

One of the highlights of Christchurch for me was the daily entertaining rants in the Cathedral Square of the old man, famously known as 'the Wizard'. He is an eccentric old man who stands in the square daily at about 1.00 pm, dressed head to toe in a full wizard outfit complete with pointy hat, as he pontificates on topics such as God, women and life in general. His only prop is a stepladder, which he occasionally climbs to add emphasis to his presence and his transport is a bright red VW Beetle, which is actually made from the front ends of two cars, welded together.

I'm not usually one for paying any attention to those slightly fanatical and very annoying people who insist on preaching their beliefs at you in public, while you try to get on with your shopping and ignore them, but the Wizard is altogether a different kind of crazy. He is more like a one-man, random comedy act and reminded me a little of a slightly more intellectual, older version of Billy Connelly, but without the swearing. His almost chauvinistic views on women are more funny than offensive and I could have happily planned each day around his forty-five minutes of philosophising for sheer amusement value.

Still, we had bigger fish to fry as they say, or in our case swim with (and I know they're technically not fish, but 'we had bigger mammals to fry' just doesn't make sense). So after getting the bus to Kaikoura, we booked onto the afternoon trip with Dolphin Encounter and got ready for what I would say was undoubtedly the ultimate highlight of New Zealand.

I know people who have swam with dolphins in captivity, my own dad has pictures of him being carried by two across a pool in Florida and he absolutely loved it. But, I cannot imagine another more astounding, totally incredible experience than swimming in the wild with hundreds of them all around you.

After being kitted out with wet suits, masks and snorkels, we had a briefing about how to act and what to do to get the most out of our time in the water. The crew would track the pods of dusky dolphins and drop us into the water in front of them as they swam, so that when they reached us we'd have several minutes with them swimming all around.

We were told that to get the best interaction from the dolphins, we should make as much movement and noise as possible, as they are apparently very curious and will want to check out anyone that seems interesting to them. I have to say I was a little sceptical when they suggested that singing, squealing and thrashing about in the water would attract the best attention and envisaged being ridiculed at how silly we all looked, having fallen for what was surely a set-up.

So, when we were given the signal to drop into the water, I stuck my head under the surface and watched, holding my breath with anticipation and feeling a little vulnerable hanging in the water, waiting to be checked out by a group of reasonably large creatures. But, as soon as they came into view, I was blown away. There were quite literally hundreds of them, five hundred or so as we later found out, belonging to not one, but two pods.

They literally surrounded us and were swimming in every direction in pairs, groups, on their own and under us, around us and even jumping over us out of the water so you didn't know which way to look. I soon saw that the other people in our group were taking the advice and the more noise we made and the more thrashing and turning we did, the more curious the dolphins became.

At one point, I found myself next to someone squealing Bon Jovi's 'Living on a Prayer' and I joined in as loudly and as in tune as we could. It's a pretty strange sound, two people squealing Bon Jovi, underwater, through snorkels and no surprise that I felt like a right idiot. But the feeling of foolishness vanished immediately, as three dolphins closed in and started circling us.

Unbelievably, one of them turned on its side slightly and looked us straight in the eye as it circled faster and closer and we struggled to keep up. We'd been told they might do that and not to be tempted to scare them off by reaching out, so we circled with it, locking eye contact and squealing through our snorkels, trying not to get overcome with the emotion of what was happening.

We must have circled for a good minute or two with the three dolphins and the one close enough to have touched easily. But I know that if we had tried we'd have had a much shorter encounter. As it was, the reason we lost contact was because dolphins we're not, and our ability to swim in ever-decreasing circles is significantly lacking. So our new friends took one last look at us, before swimming off and leaving us absolutely awestruck.

As the dolphins left and we surfaced for the first time, I discovered that the other person was my university friend Michelle and we just hugged and carried on squealing, but this time with sheer excitement and wonder. It was the most amazing experience and one I'll never ever forget. The dolphins are just the most graceful, playful creatures with the kindest faces and they almost seem to smile at you. We watched them from the boat as we made our way back and they put on a show for us, jumping and diving over each other and playfully somersaulting until they disappeared out of sight.

That was my closing experience of New Zealand and as we returned to Christchurch all we had left to do was prepare for our journey home. I think that to say I was ready to go home gives the impression that I'd had enough travelling and I don't think that will ever be the case. I was ready to change into some clean clothes and to see my family and friends and I also think that four months of amazing experiences is enough in one go. For me, any longer and I start to reach saturation point and stop getting as much out of each new place as I would with a fresh pair of eyes.

So I returned to Heathrow once again and was once again met by my very excited family, whom I am always thrilled to see. I have since bought my first property and discovered that once a homeowner, bricks and mortar seem to construct a bottomless money pit and my scope for travel for several months on end is somewhat decreased. Still, there's more than one way to skin a cat as they say, and plenty more than one way to travel the world.

Colombia 2008

Rotary International and world Spanish - the basics

In an average Colombian day there are two bank robberies, eight highway robberies, eighty seven murders and 204 assaults or muggings. If you survive the seven and a half mile ride into Bogotá from the airport, be warned that crime is prevalent in the vicinity of hotels and bars and should you be victimized then expect little sympathy from the Police or military who are busy covering their own asses from the threat of terrorism, drug cartels and crime lords. It's no surprise Colombia ranks in Robert Young Pelton's* *The World's Most Dangerous Places*.

(*Robert Young Pelton. ComeBackAlive.com. World's most dangerous places 2006 – 2010)

'Me llamo Sally, tengo treinta y cinco anos y soy de Inglaterra. Mis pasatiempos son correr, el buceo, pasando tiempo con mis amigos y viajar. Visito muchos paises incluyendo Australia, Canada, Nueva Zelanda, Ejipto y muchos otros, pero esta es mi primera visita a Sud America.'

[My name is Sally, I am thirty-five years old and I live in England. My pastimes are running, diving, spending time with my friends and travelling. I have visited many countries including Australia, Canada, New Zealand, Egypt and many more, but this is my first visit to South America.]

That was just a snippet of my part of the group presentation we had to give more than fourteen times, to different Rotary Clubs during our travels through Colombia. At this point, it is probably worth adding that Colombia is not one of those countries where English is widely spoken and you can get by, confident in the knowledge that at least someone will be able to help you out. They speak Spanish and not the European dialect either and they are very proud of their culture. Until

May 2008, when I flew to Colombia I spoke very little Spanish, in any dialect.

I first heard of Rotary International when a family friend who is part of the organisation travelled to Sri Lanka after the tsunami, to help rebuild a local school there. But, to be honest other than that I, like most other people I have since spoken to, assumed that Rotary was similar to the Masons. I envisaged their using funny handshakes and that you had to be invited into an elite businessman's club through some bizarre initiation ceremony that involved drinking the blood of a sacrificial pig and chanting some ancient mantra.

But the Rotary Club – and probably the Masons in reality – isn't like that at all and is actually full of very normal, very charitable people who predominantly use their time to raise money and awareness for charities across the world. For example, Rotary International are instrumental in the eradication of polio in many developing countries and they do an amazing amount for small charitable organisations, while taking an active part in providing aid for greater mass disasters worldwide.

Rotary International also recognises the huge importance of creating links between cultures all over the world, promoting awareness of international issues and using these relationships to work together to achieve a common understanding and partnership working. It was through such an initiative, namely the Group Study Exchange (GSE) that I was fortunate enough to travel to Colombia, one of the most fascinating countries I have ever visited.

The GSE programme is something that is supported through Rotary clubs around the UK and the world alike. It offers young professional people the opportunity to visit other countries and learn about their cultures on a vocational visit, while promoting Rotary. The scheme is open to people aged between twenty-five and forty, in a professional occupation, who have no prior connection to Rotary. So, when I heard about a trip to Bogotá, I immediately jumped at the opportunity to find out as much as I could about it and was fortunate enough to be selected as one of four professionals, including Anne, Kate and my friend and colleague Steve, in a team with a Rotarian leader.

However, as well as embarking on a finely tuned programme of vocationally orientated visits and sightseeing, we were to be very much representatives for our country and for Rotary. Part of that relatively formal commitment was to deliver presentations to each hosting Rotary club about our country, our jobs and ourselves. Not forgetting that this is essentially a non-English-speaking country and all of the presentations were to be in Spanish, which none of us spoke!

We would also be staying with different Colombian families, all from different Rotary clubs, who were to act as our hosts. So in January 2008, we began the process of crash learning enough basic Spanish to at least get us by.

I have to admit, that even at the time we boarded our flight from Heathrow in May 2008, I had only a rough idea of what the trip would be like. I knew from speaking to people who had been on previous exchanges that it would be hard work, with a tight and hectic schedule and that we would be undertaking a lot of formal visits and be the guests at different Rotary meetings daily. I also knew I couldn't wait and that because this was a country I could never envisage myself visiting as a tourist, I would never get another opportunity like it again.

Bienvenido de Bogotá

It was approximately 9.30 pm local time when we landed in Bogotá to the heaviest torrential rain I think I have ever seen. We collected our bags and headed to the arrivals lounge anticipating our first introduction to our hosts and perhaps a general briefing about the next four weeks. But as it turned out, nothing in Colombia or about that trip was predictable or like anything else I have ever experienced before.

Quite literally the second we stepped foot onto the tarmac outside the exit door we were each grabbed by a different pair of hands, hugged tightly, kissed and subjected to an onslaught of excited, advanced and totally incomprehensible Spanish. We were then each grabbed by every other member of our welcoming party in turn, until we had met each one, were completely disorientated and were then whisked off with barely enough time to understand that we were being taken to our individual host families, or to say goodbye.

It took no more than fifteen minutes from the first hug to being driven away in the back of a stranger's car, in a country I had never been to before and to be honest, had actually only ever heard negative reports about. I remember staring out of the back window into the driving rain and wondering what had just happened and whether I should be worried if I was ever going to see the rest of my group again.

As I sat in the back of the car with my Rotary host and new Colombian *hermana* (sister) Sonia in the front, with her sister Claudia, they chatted away to me in Spanish that I had trouble keeping up with and barely understood. I started to wonder what I had got myself into and doubted that being able to say my name, count to one hundred and ask the way to the airport would be enough to see me through the next four weeks.

We drove through a quiet and rain-drenched city and I noticed that we rarely stopped at red traffic lights and often drove in the centre, rather than at the sides of the roads. I assumed, as you do when you arrive somewhere new, that this must be a quirky form of alternative road discipline, or that they were simply exceptionally bad drivers. I soon learned that Bogotá unfortunately does still have very real issues of road crime and street violence in some areas, so it is generally accepted that you don't drive with less than two people in the car at night and, where safe, you do not always stop at red lights.

I also noticed during the journey to my family's home that many of the residential streets in Bogotá have security systems of varying degrees. They range from having guards at the main entrance to an estate to wrought-iron gated communities, with each house protected by a locked gate and each street with an armed guard and secure entrance.

When we arrived at our gated house in the secure street of a reasonably wealthy area, I was greeted by Sonia's mother who is one of the most hospitable, welcoming and vivacious women I have ever met and from that point on was, *Mi mami en Colombia*. However, while Sonia and her sister mercifully spoke very good English, *mi mami en Colombia* didn't, not a word. She did however speak very fast Spanish and seemed to have no concept of the fact that I didn't speak it to at least degree level, so most of the time I had absolutely no idea what she was saying.

Mami had cooked for my arrival, which was 5.00 am by my body clock and the last thing I felt like doing was eating. But, another thing I soon learned about the Colombians is that they extend their hospitality by offering food and it almost borders on offensive if you don't partake when offered. I also wanted to spend some time with these lovely people who had welcomed me into their home and seemed so excited by my being there.

So, at ridiculous o'clock we sat down to a buffet of hot empanadas, which are small pasty-type delicacies filled with meat and vegetables, and a cold bean salad. I had my first taste of real Colombian food, which amusingly wasn't wholly different to a Cornish pasty and real Colombian conversation, of which I'd say I understood one word in what felt like every hundred or so.

I eventually went to the bedroom Sonia had given up for me and looked out of the window at the surrounding houses. The properties that backed onto our terrace were a matter of only a few metres away and separated by tiny spaces with corrugated iron roofs, forming makeshift outside areas. I remember thinking then, what a different culture I was living in and how that even in a relatively wealthy area, the impact of the country's historic problems was still very real.

By the time I went to bed I was overwhelmed with excitement, exhaustion and intrigue at my new surroundings and I think it would be fair to say, well and truly out of my comfort zone.

Ron and salsa - strictly in that order

The briefing we were anticipating when we first arrived in Colombia happened on our first morning in Bogotá when I went downstairs to find mami was looking after me for the day. Mami was a fabulous character and talked incessantly to me while making flamboyant hand gestures and giggling like a coy teenage girl. Our conversations consisted mostly of her talking and me desperately trying to search for a word I recognised. There weren't many, so I improvised by watching her body language and facial expressions, to get some indication of the face I should pull to acknowledge I had at least a vague notion of the tone of what she was saying.

Our welcome to Rotary in Colombia was very touching and as we sat in the home of one of our hosts, we were treated to a wonderfully warm introduction and, of course, lunch. We met many people from several of the clubs we would be visiting and learned that in each new district we would each stay with a different family, but always return to our same host families when in Bogotá.

Everyone was keen to have the opportunity to show us around and introduce us to typical foods, typical customs and of course typical salsa. The Colombians have a passion for dancing that is almost as strong as their passion for Catholicism. Not only do Colombians like to dance, but they expect that everyone dances. In fact along with learning to speak and walk, learning to dance would appear to be the third stage of child development.

Which, if you're anything like me and like to reserve dancing for situations where you are reasonably inebriated and don't actually care what you look like, or where the crowds are so thick no one can see you anyway, then it is a relative nightmare. Don't get me wrong, I love to dance with the girls on a night out after one or several pints of cider and blackcurrant (not very ladylike I realise), but I have a pathological fear of performing in front of people, hence the alcohol/crowds/dancing thing.

I don't want to give the impression of being ungrateful, but having travelled for an entire day, got to bed at our equivalent of 5.45 am and spent all day meeting and greeting, we were shattered by our first evening. All I wanted to do that first night was to go to bed and sleep to be ready for a fresh start and everything that was to come. However, the young contingents of our Rotary hosts had different ideas and were determined to show us a good Colombian night out. What can you do?

So we rallied round and found ourselves in a reasonably empty large bar, with music a little too loud to talk easily and wondering how long we'd have to stay before we could politely make our excuses. Yes, I do know I am thirty-six and not sixty-six and yes, I do realise how grouchy I sound here, but I was absolutely shattered and I put on my best sociable face, so it doesn't count.

We sat and chatted for a while, trying to overcome the language barriers as best we could and I politely declined the offer of alcohol, mentally calculating I could get away with an hour or two at the most and then we'd be good to go. The Colombians don't have a huge drinking culture, but one tipple of choice is South American rum, or 'Ron' as it is so called. Rum is not my drink of choice at the best of times and with a sleep-deprived feeling of nausea, I decided to stick to coke and do my best to make the most of the evening.

But alas before long, what would for me, soon become the dreaded sound of the first salsa dance started and almost immediately several of the Colombians jumped up. As we were the guests of honour, they eagerly picked us off one by one to partner and thankfully one of our group was an exceptionally good dancer. Having studied salsa in the UK, she was more than keen and I managed to fend off the first few dances, but figured I wouldn't be able to put off the inevitable for long.

There was only one thing left to do if I was going to be dragged up against my will onto an almost empty dance floor, so I introduced myself to Ron. Ron and I watched, cringing at memories of being dragged on to a similarly empty dance floor to undergo the torture of being made to dance with my dad at family weddings. I never knew the steps, had no idea what I was doing and spent most of the time treading on his toes, but sadly, not in that cute way that little girls sometimes do with their dads.

The Colombian music though was fantastic and as the bar gradually filled and the dance floor became crowded, so the atmosphere became vibrant. There were even people in costumes on stilts at one point and it reminded me, not of a dull family party, but more of a miniature carnival. The music played, people danced and Ron and I became very well acquainted. In fact, Ron was such a good influence on me that he had me up and dancing before very long at all and the night went from there.

I won't lie and pretend that it wasn't embarrassingly awkward at first. Nor will I try to suggest that an equal number of people were as keen to dance with me as they were with Anne, who did know the difference between a salsa and a reggaeton. But all I will say is, I held my own in quantity if not quality and by 3.00 am, local time, I was the last English person standing and was eventually, reluctantly, dragged home.

Tastes of Colombia

We started early the following day and to my delight, I woke without a hangover, I loved Ron! Our hosts wanted to show us the sights of Bogotá and as they are an extremely religious population, our first outing was to the Monserrate Cathedral, which sits at 3,000 metres above sea level. In fact, the whole capital city sits within the Andes at 1,600 metres above sea level, so you can already feel the difference in altitude just by walking along the street.

As we arrived at the base of the mountain which hosts the cathedral, we saw for the first time the level of security on the streets during the day. There were groups of 'Policía' and military personnel, heavily armed and gathered in groups as a high-profile presence, to protect the general public from whatever dangers still pose such a significant threat. It was a little unnerving at first, but somehow like the armed guards in the residential areas, they soon became a familiar sight.

After a cable car ride up the very steep mountain, we walked to the summit and had to take time to catch our breath. The cathedral itself was beautiful, but not being a religious girl, I was just as interested in the street markets and stalls on the cobbles outside. Most markets have a selection of mediocre gifts, bargains and, if you're lucky the odd truly unique find, but there is usually also a lot of tat. Still, in a market within the grounds of a prominent cathedral, I didn't expect the tat to be positively sacrilegious.

To our amusement, among countless tacky, cheaply decorated statues of Christ in numerous vulgar poses, we found several paintings of Jesus on his cross, laying in the path of a looming metro car, typical of one of Bogotá's street cable routes. I wouldn't be surprised if somewhere in Colombia there is now an artist lying in the street having been unexpectedly struck down by a freak lightning bolt, testament to some form of divine retribution.

No matter where you go in Colombia, people everywhere seem to want to make you eat or drink something. So, in the interests of being polite, we found ourselves drinking some rather potent-smelling hot liquid that resembled dishwater with herb-like bits floating on the surface. It turned out to be a coffee-flavoured drink made with real coffee beans, some herb-like bits and the staple alcoholic beverage in Colombia, *aguardiente* which directly translated means firewater. You're never going to be onto a winner drinking copious amounts of anything called firewater, the name giving the obvious impression it's not easy on the palate, so we opted for one drink and left.

The rest of our first afternoon was spent wandering the streets of Bogotá and getting a real feel for the city. The roads and streets are quite poorly kept and a lot of the buildings in some state of disrepair. If you go into any building with several storeys, you can look out onto the corrugated iron roofs of the more lowly properties and see how closely packed everything is. The police and military have a very high presence, but are surprisingly low key and the people are amazingly friendly. There is a stark lack of what the Colombians refer to as white people in the country and almost no tourism. Due to the violent history and drug trafficking, tourists have long been dissuaded from visiting Colombia and tend to pass it by for more popular South American countries.

There is also sadly a lot of poverty in the city and surrounding villages and towns and it is heart wrenching to see the severely disabled or even young children wandering through the static traffic or at the sides of the road selling just about anything. Many of them are what are termed *displacados* and are the result of the guerrillas raiding their hillside villages, killing and kidnapping, trying to recruit into their cause. The only way for the people to avoid being murdered or losing their children to the militia is to flee their homes and go to the larger cities and try to scrape a living by selling what they can make or find.

The streets are also littered with street sellers, mostly selling fruits or snacks and we had great fun sampling all the various delicacies. My favourite had to be without a doubt the most disgusting-looking fruit I have ever seen in my life, but it tasted delicious. The granadilla (sometimes rather aptly referred to as 'snot fruit') is about the size of a large peach and very light in weight. It feels hollow and has a firm shell-like skin, which is a sort of green yellow colour. The way to eat it is to smash it against something and then literally suck out the contents, which are transparent, pea-sized and jelly-like balls with all the consistency and visual appeal of frogspawn. Delicious, if you can get over the fact you're eating what essentially looks like frogspawn!

Everywhere we went in Colombia, they have a dish that is *typical de region* and therefore we were lucky enough to be treated to plenty of delicious food. However, they're not big vegetable eaters with dinner and meals tended to mainly consist of some of the largest hunks of meat I've ever seen without any legs attached, or fish. There would usually be an accompanying *platano*, which is a large savoury banana, or some steamed rice and the occasional parsnip-style vegetable, or salad.

Unfortunately for us though, it seems that a countrywide favourite was a sweet, rather sickly and, in my opinion, thoroughly unpleasant combination of caramel toffee, jam and cheese fused together in a trio of sticky layers and forced on us at any and every opportunity. They eat a version of it for dessert, melted down into a gooey paste, or just as a sweet wrapped in cellophane and they go absolutely mad for it. The trouble is, when you've accepted something once and politely pretended you like it, it becomes increasingly difficult to explain in broken Spanish how you actually don't. So, we became increasingly adept at inventively disposing of the offending sweet wherever we went.

That first week was spent pretty much acclimatising to the altitude and being shown a 'tourist's guide' to Bogotá and easing in gently. We did one presentation to the rotary club of our Colombian trip organiser, Raimundo and despite ridiculous nerves, it seemed to go well. Although, I'm not so sure having two members of the audience fall asleep mid-flow is a positive sign.

We also visited the *Minas de Sal*, which is a vast underground salt mine in the hills and, unbelievably, hosts a hugely cavernous and working cathedral. There were actually people sitting on rows and rows of pews, waiting for a service as they faced an imposingly tall cross, carved out of the salt face. As I said before, I'm not a religious person, but it was undoubtedly an impressive sight and I couldn't help marvelling at the rows of people all dimly lit by the thousands of candles, just waiting and praying. Still, unaffected by the spirituality of the setting, I got my own kicks from joining all the other non-believers in marvelling at caves made entirely of salt and mindlessly licking the walls. I kid you not.

The hospitality of the Colombians was like nothing I have ever experienced before - so warm and amazingly generous. We spent the rest of the day at the *finca* of one of the host families, which is their country residence set in the beautiful mountain countryside. The house was fantastic, set in rolling hills with a stunning lakeside position and acres of orchards and exotic flowers to wander through after dinner.

Needless to say, dinner was obviously the main focus of the afternoon and was of course a meal *typical de region*. To start, we had a rather comical attempt at preparing the plantains by quite literally stomping them into pancakes. The banana-like fruit is huge and cut into slices and then placed on a sheet of plastic on the floor. Another layer of plastic then goes on top of the plantain and a wooden board on top of that. The fun bit then comes when you stand on top of the board and basically do the twist, preferably while holding onto someone for support. The very flat banana pancake is then prised from the floor and fried in a mixture of oil, garlic, lemon and tastes delicious. The size of pancake being directly proportional to the weight of the person doing the twist!

The main course was probably one of my favourite Colombian meals, a cream-based soup into which they spoon fluffy rice, chicken, capers and avocado, eaten with a salad and corn on the cob accompaniment. This brings us nicely on to dessert or not so nicely, considering it was yet again another jam/cheese/caramel gooey splat and not so easily disposed of under the eager stares of our hosts.

The real Colombia

After that first few days of acclimatising and being essentially tourists, the real work began and we started to get some insight into Colombia's changing history, the tragedies its people have suffered and the steps they have taken to make their country into a place to be proud of.

Unfortunately to do all of this, our days invariably started at anything between 5.00 and 7.00 am and lasted anywhere from fourteen to twenty hours. Our timetable always began with breakfast with our host family. As it appeared to be an offence punishable by death to even try to skip a meal in Colombia, abstaining for an extra half an hour in bed was never an option. We'd then do between two and six visits in a day, as well as meeting various new host rotary clubs and their particular host families, giving our presentations in Spanish to them over a formal lunch and dinner and then partaking in whatever night-time entertainment they had arranged in our honour.

We knew that we were there in Colombia with Rotary to promote Rotary International and build relationships between the two cultures and to be good ambassadors for our country. What I didn't anticipate was the high regard in which we would be held on every one of our visits and the staggering generosity lavished upon us as if we were VIPs, wherever we went.

Our tour started at the Escuela de Cadetes de Policía General Santander, which is the National Police Academy for Police Officers in Colombia, based in Bogotá. The police force has a very military-like structure in both rank and discipline, but is civilian based and has very stark differences to that in the UK.

We were greeted by the Colonel and second in command of the academy, who introduced a small team of designated officers who would accompany him in giving us a guided tour. We then met the General who presides over the entire academy and is personally responsible for enforcing the military-like discipline among the officers on site. We sat for coffee in a very polished and adorned boardroom, surrounded by photographs of historic police figureheads, medals and flags and the obligatory painting of the King. It was all very formal and serious and I realised that we were in a very privileged position. I started to wish I hadn't opted for the more casual of the two uniforms we had – or worn open-toed sandals with red nail varnish.

As the Colonel and his team took us around the academy we took photographs, asked plenty of questions and marvelled at the differences compared to our own police training centres and headquarters. The pride in every single little detail was impressive, from the sculpted grounds and polished brass plaques adorning every building, to the immaculate uniform and military-like way the officers marched around the site. In fact, quite amusingly, one of the General's new rules was for all officers to immediately break into a jog in the presence of any higher-ranking officer, while saluting in their direction. Given that we were with the second highest-ranking officer at the academy, you'd think the novelty of seeing young, eager to please officers break into an awkward run and anticipating the odd stumble would wear off, but I have to admit the devil in me found it consistently quite amusing.

I really couldn't believe the effort that had been made to give us the best possible insight into the academy and the lengths they had gone to welcome us. We had people running around in front of us to open doors, plying us with refreshments at every opportunity and performances from several departments, including the horses, dogs, brass band and a tour of the armoury. They even have a section in ceremonial dress that sing and dance at formal events and they had compiled and performed a song for us, with the chorus in English especially for our visit. We had a three-course meal with waitress service and danced with the performers and spent a great deal of the time looking at each other wide-eyed and marvelling with wonder at what we had done to deserve such treatment.

I honestly felt almost guilty, as if they had gone to all this trouble under the misconception that someone far more important was coming and that at any moment they might cotton onto the fact it was just 'little old us' and throw us out as impostors.

One of my personal most lasting memories of the police academy was the stark difference between the regulations for women compared to those in the UK. We learned that one of the directives from the General was for the women to wear well-applied and tasteful make-up and a polished court shoe with a little heel at all times while in uniform. Their bed spaces and living quarters had to be brightly coloured and adorned with girly accessories such as teddy bears, butterflies and pretty posters and all in order for them to stay in touch with their femininity while in training! I dread to think what impression the Colombians would have of British policewomen in their generic uniforms with steel toe-capped boots and unflatteringly, emasculating trousers.

Spanglish

When you don't speak the language in a country that predominantly doesn't speak any English, you have to get by somehow and do your best. Our Spanish was improving every day and I could feel myself getting braver and more confident as my accent improved. But, inevitably there were limitations and we were forced at times to develop a sort of half-Spanish, half-English dialect. This Spanglish arose from getting halfway through any given sentence and having to substitute Spanish for English to finish the sentence in any way you could. It also involved a great deal of hand gesturing, facial expressions and any form of body language necessary to get the gist of the conversation across. It's a bit like charades, but three times longer and a lot more frustrating.

We no doubt understood more than we could speak and as we had only learned a limited vocabulary, we became adept at certain conversations about very particular topics. Our conversations seemed to form a pattern, starting with how much we liked Colombia, how fabulous the food had been, what we thought of the people and country, compared to our perceptions prior to visiting and how cold and wet it is in the UK and after the hundredth time, yawn!

Very mundane, but having any conversations outside these subjects proved to be quite tricky, as I found out with one host family in Sogamoso, in the district of Boyacá. This particular family were incredibly friendly and gentle and very warm and welcoming, though none of them spoke a single word of English. Somehow we managed to have a conversation about all sorts of things, including their telling me about their son and his family in the USA, their daughter in Spain and their other son who had unfortunately died at the age of thirty. I was suitably sympathetic and tried my best to offer my best words of concern and condolence to their seeming surprise and confusion. It wasn't until the following morning at breakfast when their 'dead' son walked in very much alive, that I realised I'd somehow got the wrong end of the stick and to this day, I have absolutely no idea what they had actually been talking about.

Still, on the plus side, we were a constant source of amusement to our fellow Colombians who weren't used to English speakers or any form of outside tourists. So, in times of total desperation, I soon realised I could resort to just randomly pointing at things and naming the ones I knew in my best Spanish. I found this technique particularly useful when on any form of car journey and subsequently restricted in the use of body language or gesturing for added emphasis. They go mad for it because they think you're learning new words, but in actual fact randomly pointing and excitedly naming 'sheep' 'cow' and 'tree' is a bit like being three again, but with the added humiliation of not actually being three.

The Colombians drive like the Vietnamese – only seemingly more recklessly given that the roads are 1,600 metres above sea level and there is invariably a sheer drop to one side. As there is no train system in Colombia, most of the haulage is done by road through the mountains via very large, very fast juggernauts. The downside is that when you are in a relatively small car, it gets rather hairy every time you come face to face with a lorry overtaking another lorry on a blind bend and you find that for a split second, you're actually contemplating the chances of surviving the impending plummet versus the head on collision. It seems of no great concern to the Colombians though, because most vehicles display a mini statue or photo of the Virgin Mary somewhere near the driver, which is supposed to bring them safe travel on the roads. Somehow I think their chances would be greatly improved if they stopped relying on divine intervention and simply drove more carefully.

Another amusing experience was the daily encounters with new Rotary groups at various different meeting points. We'd arrive after several hours of travelling, usually at an arranged service area and no sooner than the vehicle's engine stopped, we'd be descended upon by a hoard of people babbling in advanced Spanish. The doors would be opened and we'd be hugged and ushered towards a car with our bags barely following us before being piled into a vehicle and whisked away.

It may sound very random, but that's exactly what it was like and the only way we'd know they were actually Rotarians was by a small gold pin badge on a tie or lapel and the fact that they seemed to know our names. Most of the time we hadn't a clue where we were going first, whether we'd be seeing the other members of our group once we got there or who was in fact our host in the new group. On more than one occasion, I found myself marvelling how in a country that once had the world's highest kidnapping rate, I was doing an awful lot of jumping into random vehicles with complete strangers and assuming everything would be fine.

Colombia yesterday, today and tomorrow

Colombia is divided into thirty-two departments, which are the equivalent of what we call counties. Since the nineteenth century, it has been a country racked with civil war and political violence, including the bloodshed of *La Violencia* in the 1950s and the paramilitary and guerrilla warfare that followed.

The remote and fertile soils and climate also provide the perfect conditions for growing bountiful harvests of coca and marijuana. By the mid-1960s, drug smuggling was a very serious business in Colombia. Colombia was responsible for nearly 80 per cent of the cocaine making its way to the United States by the 1980s.

Our commitments in Colombia took us through several different departments and allowed us to meet so many different people and Rotary groups that we had to keep a daily diary in order to remember each experience. I won't recount every single day, but suffice it to say, our experiences were different in each new place and gave us insight into the many different sides to Colombia.

Without wishing to sound ungrateful to our hosts, it did become apparent that we were being very much shrouded from the potential dangers that are still very evident in the country. We weren't permitted to go anywhere without a chaperone. There are still certain areas of the countryside and even some cities that are off limits due to the history of drugs and violence and we saw some very disturbing examples of poverty.

Every day was so full of activities that we barely had a minute to ourselves and with everyone new that we met wanting to spend time with us and show us around, there was no time for rest. When we first left Bogotá to travel to the district of Boyacá we were up at 5.00 am and into the minibus, which arrived three hours later at a military arms manufacturer. We were descended upon in the usual fashion by our hosts and whisked through the dusty hot car park into the factory. At each new place they were so hospitable, offering us drinks and snacks and a full lunch and then we had a tour of the plant.

I've never seen anything like the factory we explored that day and it seemed sort of surreal. The plant was one of the country's largest producers of official weapons and ammunition, with a production of over US$1 million per year and they supply only Colombian police and military. They make every single intricate component in exactly the same way, by pouring molten wax into moulds to make wax models of the component. The wax is then cooled and coated in seven layers of clay and plaster before that is left to cool and set. The whole thing is then placed in a furnace so that the wax melts away and produces a ceramic negative mould.

The next stage is for steel to be heated to over 1,500 degrees Celsius and poured into the mould, which then sets and voilà you have a weapon or component thereof. It was a fascinating procedure to watch at each stage and it sort of felt a bit like one of those Blue Peter features you used to watch on TV as a kid, but without the risk assessment. I have to say, as fascinating as it was, I had another one of those bizarre reality checks at the point when our group of about fifteen was standing a mere six feet away from the man pouring the 1,500 degree Celsius molten steel, without us having any protective clothing, screens or seemingly any consideration whatsoever to health and safety.

Imagine going anywhere in the UK where some bloke is melting steel within feet of a group of tourists as they jump out of the way of random sparks of red hot metal, while trying not to sustain third-degree burns. I had to giggle at such a rudimentary set-up, but soon had the smile wiped from my face by the shock of a close encounter with one of those hot sparks and we swiftly moved on.

By now, we were quite accomplished at giving our presentations in Spanish to whichever Rotary club we were attending and they usually followed dinner at the relevant club's formal meeting. Most people that know me well enough know that one of my worst fears in life is public speaking – or public anything to be honest. I hate doing anything where lots of people are watching me. The positive part of presenting in Spanish was that we had no choice but to stick to the pre-prepared script and although we impressed everyone with our obviously newly learned Spanish, we weren't proficient enough to take questions or ad lib, which for me made it much less nerve-racking.

Most of the presentations were also given at formal dinners or lunches. Even when we weren't dining formally, our Colombian hosts just couldn't resist the opportunity to feed us, anytime, anywhere. We went to one small and very pretty town called Tibasosa, which is apparently the home of the Feijoa. A Feijoa is a small green fruit, which looks like a cross between a kiwi and a lime and tastes like neither. However, when you're in the largest producing area of anything, there is no escape and we found ourselves almost being force-fed. We tried Feijoa juice, which was delicious, Feijoa cake, Feijoa liqueur (which is never going to sit well on top of cake and juice) and eventually the raw version, straight from its skin. I have to confess, if I never see another Feijoa again!

After another hair-raising journey through the Andes, our next stop was Nobsa for a quick lunch and presentation and then onto the town of Tunja, still in the Boyacá district. One of the most enlightening visits we had in Colombia came in Tunja, at the Primera Brigada, which is a branch of the military and has the responsibility of tackling the drug traffickers and guerrillas in the outlaying plains. Historically, the drug trade has had a huge impact on the violence within the country villages and in the cities.

We learned that since 2004, the forces in Tunja have made amazing progress in the fight against the narco traffickers and the guerrillas and it is now the safest department in Colombia. The guerrillas now control less than half of the land they used to and there were no kidnappings in Tunja in 2005, 2006 or 2007. In partnership with the police, the Primera Brigada work to completely eradicate kidnappings, narco traffickers and paramilitary killings and are working towards the forces being able to patrol the streets of Tunja weapon-free by 2020.

We continued the law enforcement theme with a visit to a local police station in Boyacá and were once again amazed with the resourcefulness of a community with so much hardship and adversity. Along with the countrywide issues and history of violence, we learned that one of the main problems faced by the local police in Colombia is domestic violence. There is a cultural acceptance of male dominance in Colombia and the men folk are renowned for extramarital affairs and then leaving the mothers of their many children high and dry. This issue, coupled with copious amounts of alcohol, invariably leads to the vengeful wrath of numerous wronged women and the backlash from their men. In short, we were told it is sort of a domestic time bomb in a lot of Colombian families.

However, quite amazingly for a country with such hugely demanding widespread problems and large-scale issues, they seemed to have a humbling attitude to local community concerns and lifestyles. For example, the local community police fund and run a scheme where they educate and assist families to grow their own produce and be more self-sufficient to promote a sense of community and improved lifestyle.

Just keep smiling...

After an early start in Tunja and several morning visits, we spent the day with a newly established Rotary club who thankfully took us to a pizzeria for lunch and had a much more relaxed attitude to our being there. We were taken to a shopping mall, introduced to their families and spent all afternoon relaxing around their homes, being welcomed like old friends. As usual, we had very little idea of our schedule and only had a pre-prepared agenda with place names and whether we were to be there during the morning or afternoon as our guide. We had become quite accustomed to just going with the flow and accepting that 'Colombian time' is without any parameters and things were pretty much organised around us on a very flexible timetable.

However, we were eventually piled into two cars and waved off with a quick blessing from the wife of one of our drivers. I wasn't filled with great confidence though, as her blessings were apparently conditional and having made the sign of the cross at each person in turn she promptly dismissed me when she learned I was a non-believer and my fate sat quite simply in the hands of our driver.

So, we were driven the hair-raising two-hour journey through the mountains to our next meeting place, where we arrived to find we were more than two hours late and our receiving hosts looked less than impressed. As we parked and got out of the cars outside what looked like a country hotel, the Rotarians filed out in smart dress and stood around staring at us, with barely more than a few nods for welcome.

Fortunately one of the new group spoke good English and we apologised profusely, hoping that she would be able to make them understand that we had little control over our agenda. Whether it was accepted or not I don't know, but they seemed intent on pressing on with the evening's affairs and just as intent on not letting us out of their sight for a minute, lest we further hamper the proceedings. So after literally following us to the hotel rooms we were to share for the night and waiting impatiently outside while we had just enough time to dump our bags and nip to the toilet, they then whisked us into the function room for another formal dinner.

The dinner was pleasant, if a little strained, from our awkward arrival and the fact we were absolutely shattered. That was one of the longest days for us and one of the few times I remember having to really make an effort to be sociable and not let the cracks show. We made it through dinner and politely chatted with the group hoping that they would be sympathetic to our haggard appearances and allow us an early night. But alas our late arrival was not easily forgiven and apparently hell hath no fury like a Rotary club scorned. So, without further negotiation, it was decided that we would accompany the hardcore party people of Moniquirá Rotary Club to a local night spot where I can only assume they thought they were giving us our first taste of salsa – oh dear God!

Unnervingly again, the club was initially quite empty, with the few occupants being the wrong side of what I guessed to be at least fifty, our hosts included. But, they were after all Colombian and there was music playing, which meant only one thing, I needed Ron. It was quite obvious by this stage in the trip that the two other girls in our group were quite prepared to throw themselves into the whole salsa scene with no more encouragement than a funky beat and a willing partner. However, Steve and I needed a little warming up before hitting the dance floor and with mutual intuition we went in search of Ron.

I don't know if it was too much Ron, the uncharacteristic smoking of what I assume was tobacco with some of the Colombians outside the club throughout the night, or only four hours' sleep, but I can't remember ever having a worse hangover than when we were forced out of bed at 7.00 am the next morning. In fact, as most of my friends know, I notoriously suffer with ridiculously debilitating hangovers and on a particularly bad day am good for nothing until at least twenty-four hours later. But I knew it was going to be a really bad one when I realised I could hardly support my own head and then nearly fell out of the shower.

When you're feeling delicate, there are few things you want to do other than laying in bed, preferably in a darkened room, keeping as still and as quiet as possible, with the only thing passing your lips being cold water in copious quantities. But, what occurred throughout the rest of that day can only be described as hell on earth. I'm not a God-fearing person, but if I have ever believed there was some sort of higher being with an agenda, he had unbridled torture planned for me that day.

After dragging my sorry backside out of bed, I put on a fixed smile and my biggest shades and did my best to avoid standing within sniffing distance of any Rotarian likely to detect the alcohol exuding from my every pore. I steeled myself for one of the most challenging days yet and had absolutely no idea how I was going to make it through the various commitments, when I felt – and undoubtedly looked like – I'd just cheated death.

To my horror when we went outside, it was already hot and without a cloud in the sky it was obviously going to be a scorcher. One thing you really don't need with a killer headache and dehydration is relentless sunshine beating down on you and even less so when you have a stifling car journey through winding mountain roads ahead. Needless to say as soon as the car stopped, I had to make a controlled dash for the nearest building, which thankfully happened to be a hotel with relatively civilised toilet facilities and was the place we were due to have breakfast.

Having just cleared my stomach, the last thing I felt like doing was eating and so my nightmare continued. I could possibly have endured a slice of buttered toast or a nice fresh apple juice, but never in a lifetime of hangovers would I have ever contemplated suffering my way through a foul-smelling, greasy soup complete with lumps of slimy fat and cheesy bread. It wasn't long before I paid the facilities a second visit. I figured it couldn't get much worse and we got back in the car for the journey to our first appointment of the day.

If I had tried to imagine a worse place to visit in my state, I don't think I could have surpassed the factory that makes Colombia's favourite sweet - none other than the gooey toffee and jam-like 'delicacy' we had come to abhor. Not only was the production of the sweet the pride of the region, but they insisted on showing us every inch of that oppressively hot, sickly smelling, industrious factory and I have never wanted to get out of anywhere as quickly.

So, on the worst day of my post-drunken life, I had so far endured stifling heat, winding journeys in a car without air con, fatty soup and a claustrophobic sweet factory that smelled of sour milk. If I had slaved to compile a list of 'things I'd least want to do with a hangover' I could not have thought of anything less appealing. But it wasn't quite over yet.

As the VIP guests of Moniquirá we had a very special treat in store, prepared and rehearsed by the local school children in the enclosed, very small courtyard of their village school. So, from no more than a few feet away and with no prospect of escape, I braced myself for the final torture as they enthusiastically struck up the brass band. I'd pretty much lost the will to live by that point and so when to add insult to injury, the Colombians predictably started to dance, I detached myself from reality and joined in.

We had no choice but to brave it out and try to appear pleased to be there. With or without our hangovers, no matter where we went, all eyes were on us and as the guests of honour wherever we were, every two minutes someone somewhere took a photograph.

The beauty and the beast

One of my favourite places in Colombia has to be Villa de Leyva. It is one of the smallest but most picturesque towns we visited, set right in the Andes and with the most relaxing air. The rugged mountains form the backdrop to the white and terracotta buildings of the town, with beautiful gardens and cobbled streets at every turn. There are quaint little tavernas and restaurants with fairy lights in the trees and candles in the windows and more art galleries and gift shops than you can manage to visit.

Our host was a wonderfully jolly and friendly man named Raoul, with a funny Spanish/English accent and a warm rugged-looking face. He couldn't have been a more amiable host and instantly made us feel relaxed. We stayed in his home and in the morning went out into the nearby fields to feed the neighbour's pony. It was very early and the sun was beating down so we already knew it would be a blazing hot day. The roads were like wide tracks and there were little houses scattered along their sides with painted shutters and vivid flowers trailing down the walls. It seemed so peaceful and with the mountains looming beyond was like something from an idyllic painting. I remember looking up into the mountains that morning and marvelling at their proximity, while at the same time feeling that they should be higher and more imposing. Until someone helpfully highlighted that we were already 1,600 metres above sea level and that I wasn't exactly looking at them from the lowest point. My only disappointment about Villa de Leyva was that we couldn't spend more time there.

After returning to Bogotá and having some time with our families for one evening, we turned ourselves around for another early start and the drive to Villavicencio. We ate at an open-sided restaurant where we met our hosts and I had the largest slab of cow I think I have ever seen. Our hosts were great characters, as usual very warm and friendly and probably some of the wealthier people we stayed with.

My host was a professional woman in her late forties and impeccably turned out. The wealthier Colombian women are very dedicated to their appearance and often have surgery to enhance their looks, which is apparently very inexpensive in South America. Many older women have false nails, bouffant hair, thick make-up and are very well dressed and as Steve discovered, they seem to love English men. In fact, to my amusement, my host also took Steve under her wing when his placement fell through and seeing the way she kept staring at him, I got quite a bit of mileage from teasing him that her intentions weren't entirely honourable.

Villavicencio was seemingly the opposite of Villa de Leyva. It is a large sprawling town, bordering the plains beyond where many of the militia groups still operate. It isn't picturesque and the poverty is apparent on most of the streets, with decrepit buildings, half-dressed children and a sense of desperation that you can almost feel. It isn't safe to go out alone in Villavicencio, so the men in the group accompanied us wherever we went and there was a heavy military and police presence.

Despite the obvious poverty and sense of unsettlement in the town, I really liked Villavicencio. I felt for the first time during our trip that we were seeing the real Colombia, with an honesty and stark reality that we had been shielded from so far. Our hosts seemed keen to show us the harsh effects that the country's past has had on the present way of life and how they are struggling to do what they can to make things better for those who have suffered. We visited many different projects funded or part-funded by Rotary or other local charities and at each they watched us, looking to see our reaction to each situation and our impression of their society.

Villavicencio was where the appeal to Rotary and its international links seemed the strongest. The first project we visited was quite humbling, but also had an uplifting feel to it. It was a gentle introduction to the emotive visits that followed, but one of the places I remember as being so lovingly warm and generous. Like many of the projects, it was aimed at disabled or disadvantaged children and young people. The difference with this first one being that the users of the facility all had parents and families that supported them. The project was aimed at providing families with a centre for their disabled children to go and take part in activities, while providing support and respite for the carers.

Parents could attend with their children, but the staff there provided the care and assistance and taught the children how to thread beads, bake bread and cakes, and sing songs. Every last one of the children was so affectionate and inquisitive and the minute we stepped foot into the sparsely decorated, uncomfortably warm building, they were staring and beaming at us. Within minutes they approached us tugging at our clothes and tentatively engaging us in conversation, curious eyes wandering over our white skin and blonde hair.

As with every place we visited, they had made us gifts and presented us with hand-woven wristbands in the national colours. We learned that the three colours of the national flag – blue, gold and red – hold poignant meaning for the Colombians. The blue symbolises the ocean, lakes and skies, which are a natural beauty of the country's landscape. The gold is to remember the riches of the souls of its people and the good in the country to come and the red is to symbolise the bloodshed, forever a part of the violent history.

We stayed there for over an hour, playing with the children, eating their bread, which they eagerly served us and was actually quite tasty. As it was time to leave, they seemed genuinely sad to see us go and we were sad to leave. They cuddled us and we took photos and it was a learning experience for us to ensure that we never went out without taking our gifts with us at all times. We hadn't brought anything with us that day to present to them as we hadn't been aware we were visiting a children's project and so I left, minus a bracelet and two rings that I had been wearing when I entered and it was worth it to see their smiles.

The end of that particular day brought what I will remember for the rest of my life as one of the funniest moments of that entire trip to Colombia. The story itself is probably only mildly amusing to anyone who doesn't know the male member of our group and I am aware is possibly one of those disappointing 'you had to be there tales', but I will take a chance and tell it anyway, as it can still make me personally giggle until I lose control.

Steve is not the most butch of men and it's safe to say he's a lover, not a fighter. You may recall I mentioned that Steve and I were staying with the very well-groomed lady who had taken a mild shine to Steve and it's fair to say he was enjoying the attention, playing on the tall, dark masculine thing for all he was worth.

As we went to our rooms, I heard a loud, girly scream that any self-respecting damsel in distress would be proud of and I was more than amused to find Steve standing outside his bedroom, the door closed and flapping in a state of panic, which brought the lady of the house running. He managed to squeal, while waving his arms and hopping on the spot that a large bat had flown in the open window and was flying around his room and had swooped at his head.

It's difficult to describe the hilarity of the situation and do it justice, but suffice to say our host seemed less than impressed by such a pathetic display of panic and the two of us did nothing to help other than collapse into fits of giggles. I also quickly realised Steve had the quandary of being the only man present and therefore trying to claw back some tiny semblance of masculinity by having to deal with said distressed bat, while being absolutely scared stupid. Plus, it was also in his room so I knew that he was pretty cornered on all levels.

I wouldn't so much say he eventually plucked up the courage to go into the room, as I'm fairly sure the only reason he did was because he had no choice. But after insisting I hand him my fleece to cover his head and grabbing a broom from our host, he opened the door and looking completely ridiculous, frantically waving the broom about his head, he went in. From the performance, you'd have been quite justified in thinking the bat had a machine gun or at least twenty bat mates for back-up. But it didn't take long unfortunately to discover the room was empty again and the bat had obviously found its way back into the night air, taking Steve's dignity right along with it.

Colombia v cocaine

Until our time in Villavicencio, we'd seen only the police on the streets and the information presented to us by the military personnel who had taken the time to tell us how much Colombia had moved forward in the fight against drugs and violence. We were totally unprepared for the emotionally devastating exposure to the stark reality of what the Colombian soldiers face every day in their ongoing mission.

Our tour began with a visit to the Fiscalia, which is basically the court and magistrates' buildings and home of the Colombian equivalent to our Crown Prosecution Service. The justice system in Colombia is based on a two-tier system where a judge presides over the lower level crime and a magistrate sits for the higher level and more serious criminal cases. There has been no jury system since 1936, which is based partly on the fact that the volume of crime is simply too high to spend time on a jury-based court and also probably due to the corruption within the system, historically.

We were escorted around the Fiscalia by two armed guards, who quite literally never let us out of their sight. It was swelteringly hot in Villavicencio and coupled with the close protection, it was difficult not to feel a little claustrophobic. We had to cancel one of our visits in the morning and were simply told, 'It isn't safe.' Villavicencio is not very densely populated and because of its proximity to the outlaying plains and jungle, it is very exposed and one of the departments of Colombia that still has a big problem with the guerrilla groups.

We visited the Technical Investigation Corps (CTI), which incorporates the Serious and Organised Crime Agencies (SOCA), and leads investigation to identify the paramilitaries and guerrillas responsible for kidnappings, killings and the wide-scale violence, using forensics, phone tapping and other intelligence-based methods. We were also privileged enough to be given an appointment with the Director of the Departamento Administrativo de Seguridad (DAS) which is like Colombia's MI6. He explained that they hold all the intelligence on the narco traffickers and share it with the police and military, although we were told later that quite often that same intelligence isn't always disseminated as it should be and that each branch is guarded about protecting their own.

The visit to the VII Brigada in the afternoon, however, was the most unforgettable and emotional experience of the entire trip for me and without a doubt the memory that stands out in my mind as the most poignant. The VII Brigada is a military department, which comprises two units – one for support to transport supplies and resources to the areas where the other unit are deployed in combat against the militias.

All troops are trained in combat as they have to be prepared should the support unit be intercepted. They also have a section for community work to promote the military and the work that they are doing against the narco and anti-political causes. They also provide and promote support for rehabilitation programmes to aid physically and mentally injured soldiers and reintegrate them back into the community.

We were shown around by the Colonel, who took time to acknowledge his men wherever we went and who clearly had a great pride in his troops and the work that they do. He took us to the poor and inadequate facilities where the injured and rehabilitating men were housed and explained that they had no money to fund a new building, with more appropriate facilities. There were insufficient beds to accommodate the increasing number of troops and so the able-bodied men had willingly moved out into makeshift accommodation and tents in order for those injured men to have the drier and more comfortable quarters.

It was such a humbling experience and we almost felt embarrassed to be among such honourable people, living in such limited, poorly equipped conditions and sacrificing so much for their country.

We were taken through to the armoury and into a store where they hold all of the weapons and ammunition seized from the successful operations against the guerrillas and paramilitaries. There were racks and racks of individually tagged handguns, shotguns, automatic weapons, sawn off and adapted weapons, grenades and ammunition. We were told that the ones still in storage were awaiting pending court cases and were therefore evidence of intercepted operations and warfare.

I don't know quite what the accepted procedure for live evidence is in Colombia, or how strict are their policies on non-contamination of said evidence, but I was a little concerned when they started removing the weapons and handing us various examples for inspection. I was even less comfortable when they started taking photographs of us handling the guns, which had been seized from the guerrillas and held in a secure store, yet were to be used as court evidence, in a country historically known for its corruption. I marvelled once again at the ease with which I'd been willingly drawn into doing something I'd have ordinarily avoided.

As we walked round the base, we approached a troop of about forty men alongside a rank of motorbikes and off-road trucks. They were receiving what looked like some sort of briefing and we were told that the General was preparing them for their imminent departure into the jungle for an operation. Apparently, they had received some intelligence that a chemical drop was going to take place in the surrounding hills to provide the necessary constituent for the production of cocaine crops in that area.

Their destination was a four to five hour drive away into the jungle and they were armed and ready to go. It was almost surreal as the briefing concluded and with their General's words undoubtedly still ringing in their ears, the Colonel orchestrated a photograph of us with them and our fellow Rotarian hosts. It is so difficult to describe the conflicting feelings we felt of disbelief, angst for their imminent task and amazement at how these men were about to go to war and yet were making time to have their photographs taken with us. Then in a few sobering moments they were gone. We waved as they mounted their motorbikes, climbed into their vehicles and drove away from the base towards whatever awaited them in the jungle.

It was difficult to remain unaffected by the things we'd seen so far at the base. It was even more difficult to contemplate the reason that these men had to put their lives on the line was because of the demand for recreational drugs in the UK and many other countries far removed from the devastation caused by cocaine production.

We moved inside to a small conference room where we were seated, ready for what we anticipated to be a presentation about the successes of the operations conducted from the base. We sat in the front two rows, facing a projector screen about ten feet high and with no warning or indication of what we were about to see, the first horrific image appeared before us.

No amount of warning could have prepared us for the onslaught of gruesome and shocking photographs that the Colonel flashed on the screen one after another. He paused at each to enable us to register the images and listen to the story behind each mutilated soldier. The photographs were all equally macabre and all of soldiers who had lost or were fighting for their lives because of their injuries in the field. Most of them were injuries caused by land mines (placed in the ground by the guerrillas to protect the coca crops from intruders) and all involved dismemberments of varying degree.

It was nothing short of sickening. Yet because of the Colonel's obvious passion for the plight of his men and the reality of being there, in the very region where all of this was happening, it seemed almost disrespectful to look away. So we sat, staring at the graphic images and listening to the heart-wrenching narrative with the tears streaming down our faces. I have never felt so disturbed by anything I have witnessed or experienced before, than I felt watching those soldiers' mutilated bodies and hearing about the cause and effect of the drug trade on the Colombian people.

The presentation ended then and we were introduced to three young soldiers between twenty-three and twenty-five years old, each of who had lost a part of their legs to landmine injuries only three months before. They were on crutches and they stood in a line in front of us while the Colonel resolutely introduced them and described their individual circumstances. We listened, struggling to fight back the tears and feeling so humbled by their situation. The Colonel ended by telling us how he had spent so much time with the men injured in combat and tried to give them hope and support to get well. He described a conversation he had with one young soldier who had lost both legs and when asked whether with hindsight he would have still joined the military, the soldier said he would do it all again if it meant that his country would one day be rid of drugs and violence.

We spent the rest of the evening meeting many more soldiers and listening to their experiences and their hopes for the future. We gave a presentation, but tailored it around our positive experiences of Colombia. With the aid of a translator, we tried to impress upon the brigade how shocked we felt about what we had seen there and the sacrifices their men were making. We stressed that the message we would be taking back to England about Colombia would be a positive one and that we hoped that many more people would visit their country in the future and see for themselves what a beautiful place it is, with such amazing people.

God Save the Queen!

After our harrowing time at Villavicencio, we returned to Bogotá and thankfully had a day off to recuperate. The availability and quality of beauty salons in Bogotá is fabulous and we took the opportunity to have a manicure, pedicure, waxing and hairstyle all for the bargain equivalent of about £15.

I don't want to give any impression of being ungrateful, or negative about our time and encounters in Colombia, because it was quite simply one of the most incredible experiences of my life and I am wholly grateful to Rotary. However, it was also remarkably wearing, both emotionally and mentally. Our days were not only long and fully packed from start to finish, but we were permanently on show. We were meeting one, if not two new host Rotary clubs each day and giving our presentations at formal dinners and lunches. We were visiting so many amazing places and meeting so many interesting people, all of whom wanted to spend time with us, share experiences with us and tell us important information about their various projects. We were chaperoned wherever we went, which meant we had very little, if any, downtime and we wanted to give the best impression we could of ourselves and our country and do our best for the Rotarians who had sponsored us. But on top of all of this, most of what we said or heard was in Spanish.

By the time we reached La Vega on day seventeen, I think it's fair to say we were at breaking point. We had been promised two days off in the countryside hacienda of one of the Rotarians, but first, we had to fulfil another lunch commitment, another presentation and as was customary at most Rotary meetings, another rendition of the national and Rotary anthems.

So we stood respectfully listening to the now familiar tune and words of both Colombian anthems and then heard a more familiar melody. With amusement, fondness and a little fear, we listened as in our honour the antiquated, tinny-sounding stereo played 'God Save the Queen'. To set the scene, the Colombians stand firm to their anthem and the elder generations staunchly hold their arms across their chests in salute, while singing every last word with pride.

I think I'd struggle to get past the 'Send her victorious' verse of our anthem and as my singing abilities are reserved strictly for the shower and solitary car journeys, I hoped they weren't expecting us to perform with the same amount of vigour. Thankfully, before our lack of participation was questioned, the dodgy stereo conveniently managed to stick and after about ten repetitions of 'God Save the Queen', someone put us out of our misery and events moved on.

We spent a couple of days relaxing around the poolside villa at the hacienda, generally recharging our batteries and of course eating before we moved on to our next destination, the town of Ibagué. Ibagué is quite a large town, it doesn't have the level of problems as Villavicencio, but is still affected by the guerrilla conflict and kidnappings. The town square has huge hangings, which adorn the main buildings, displaying the faces of those who have been kidnapped, but never returned and serves as another conspicuous reminder of the problems that still exist.

Our hosts greeted us as usual and we were ferried around the city and dropped at various destinations in turn. By now, I had completely lost the will to even try to work out what was going on and just let myself be driven to wherever these new strangers cared to take me. I made the usual attempt at conversation and was surprised at how much of an improvement I seemed to be making in my pronunciation of words and how much I felt I was able to understand. We discussed the usual topics and I commented on how crazy the drivers were on the mountain roads, in particular the huge lorries that speed through the blind bends.

Now, for some reason I thought the word for lorry was something like 'mola' or similar and so mentioned it several times to emphasise my point. It seemed to invoke quite an animated reaction from one of the women, so I assumed she understood my meaning and continued blissfully unaware. In actual fact, 'mola' is a form of art from an ancient mountain tribe and so she assumed I was talking about their locally famed tapestry work. I didn't realise this until that evening's Rotary meeting where she took great delight in presenting me with a colourful and intricately stitched cloth she had brought from her own home as a gift, while pointing at it and repeating 'mola' as she eagerly watched for my appreciation. So much for my linguistic improvement!

God save Colombia

We spent the next few days at numerous facilities all in absolute dire need of further funding and development. The Fiscalia Medical Centre in Ibagué is the forensic laboratory for the analysis of all rape and murder cases in a 36,000-kilometre area. All rape victims attend that one particular centre if they make a report and need examination. There are no facilities to cater properly for traumatised victims or to enable the staff to cater for the needs of victims in such sensitive cases. Any bodies murdered by gunfire are brought to the centre, but due to lack of resources and funding they do not have X-ray facilities and so all bodies are searched by hand. If they do not find the bullet and cannot establish cause of death, they do not have the money to send the body to Bogotá and the case is closed as undetected.

There is also no facility for DNA testing at the centre and therefore if a case requires any samples to be sent to Bogotá for testing, it can take anything from six months to two years for a result to return. Only the most serious cases are sent for DNA testing, as there simply isn't the money or means to send more. The morgue was in a shocking state of disrepair, with basic facilities, dirty surfaces and pipes dripping on to the floor through light fittings.

I was totally shocked by the appalling conditions and could hardly see how any positive work could be done in such an environment. We visited a development site, where the building stood half-finished, leaking and damp and with the new walls already crumbling in places. This was supposed to be the modern facility to replace the existing centre, but it was blatantly clear that it was not even close to completion and we learned that the funding had already been depleted.

Desolation seemed to be the theme for our time in Ibagué and yet the people themselves appeared extraordinarily positive and joyful. One of the most disturbing projects was an orphanage for severely disabled children. We learned that many of them had either been orphaned when their parents were killed by guerrillas or as the victims of landmines, or perhaps more upsetting as a result of their parents having abandoned them due to the severity of the child's particular disability.

The place was sparse and the children so obviously physically and mentally impaired, but they were full of affection and delight. However, the most severe cases were confined to small classrooms with locked doors and bars on the windows and paced about, staring vacantly like caged animals. It was repulsive to see, but there were no funds or staff to improve the facility and they were desperate.

We visited numerous facilities during our stay at Ibagué, including several schools for underprivileged children, a convent-run centre for wayward girls, a rundown hospital, a rehabilitation facility for those injured by landmines where they could have prosthetic limbs fitted and a drop-in centre where volunteers hand out soya milk and food for three hundred children every day. Each project we visited made a pitch to Rotary International to appeal for aid or assistance and for us to take their message back home with us.

It never failed to amaze us how loving and happy so many of the people were, with so little. We also realised that they have a very accepting attitude to their lives and with their faith in their religion to motivate them; they just get on with it. We even saw one woman strip naked at the side of a busy road, with complete indifference to passers-by as she took advantage of a leaking water pipe to have a wash.

We did however have one other less distressing but equally interesting visit before leaving Ibagué. What trip to Colombia would be complete without an insight into the economy's greatest export and the world's finest coffee? Colombia is the world's second largest supplier of coffee after Brazil and we were fortunate enough to be taken to a local coffee plant, where they distribute 1,000 sacks of coffee per day. Each and every bag is tested and tasted and I was astonished to learn that the rejected beans stay in Colombia and become the coffee that is kept in the country for drinking.

The director of the factory informed us that around 96 per cent of the coffee produced in Colombia is exported and the Colombians, who he deemed to not have sophisticated enough palates for good coffee, are left with the dregs. He then presented us each with a decidedly questionable-looking clear bag of what he assured us was his finest coffee. However, it raised the obvious question of how we would fare at Customs, in possession of our unmarked bags of ground brown powder on our exit from the world's largest drug-producing country.

Throughout our time in Colombia, in every new town and district we visited, we would ultimately have to say goodbye to the new people we had met. Whenever you have to say goodbye, there can be an awkwardness surrounding whether you should vow to keep in touch after the time you've shared, or how you leave things without offending people. However, every goodbye was made easy for us as we merely said, '*En Paipa? Si, en Paipa!*' which basically means, 'In Paipa? Yes, in Paipa!' Paipa being the location of the Rotary District Assembly towards the end of our time in Colombia, to which almost every active Rotarian goes as if it were a pilgrimage.

We were to be the guests of honour and would face giving our final presentation to an audience of approximately five hundred. I still have no idea to this day how I managed to pull that off without passing out, humiliating myself or causing offence by fluffing my words. But, pull it off we did and the day was fantastic. We even somehow managed to get an hour or two to ourselves that afternoon, though it was no mean feat convincing several hundred chaperones that we would come to no harm if left unsupervised for the duration of one meal and a spot of shopping.

When we returned to the conference centre intact, the whole place had come alive and resembled nothing like the formally seated official venue we had left earlier that day. There were craft and art stalls lining the halls and hot and cold local traditional foods being sampled, along with the obligatory liqueur aguardiente, which we had come across several times during our stay. In fact, we soon realised that the aguardiente had clearly been flowing for some time while we'd been away and coupled with the celebratory atmosphere, most people were positively hedonistic.

Before long we were hustled into the main hall and had colourful wooden shot glasses placed round our necks on strings and immediately filled with the firewater. As most locally produced, crude regional liqueurs seem to, aguardiente tastes very strongly of aniseed and, like its name suggests, burns as it goes down. However, these commemorative little shot cups weren't just for keepsakes, as we learned very quickly. If the cup was seen dangling from its string, it clearly meant it was empty and within seconds someone, anyone, would be there, filling it up and hailing, 'Salut!' before waiting for you to knock it back in one go, ready for the next imminent refill.

The aguardiente was coming thick and fast, we were being grabbed from all angles, kissed in greeting by our hoards of previous hosts and spun around to each different tune as the salsa began. I tried at one point to buy a bottle of liqueur, but after establishing that there appeared to be no actual bar, the best I could do was try to explain to one of the Rotarians that I wanted to contribute. He scuttled off and returned within seconds with a decent-sized bottle of the clear liquid, which he persisted in opening, filling both our cups, shouting, 'Salut!' and downing the drink before shoving the bottle at me and insisting I take it without payment.

Sadly, the essential purpose of the conference was lost on us as we could barely keep up with the presentations we gave ourselves and so had little hope of understanding the majority of the rest of the speakers. But, we had absolutely no trouble understanding the party that took place that night and with festival-like music, dancers and performers and copious amounts of aguardiente, we didn't need to talk about the weather or the food once. We drank and danced and laughed and had more photos taken with more people than I care to remember, until into the small hours, when I confess I could barely stay awake.

We returned to Bogotá for a few last days with our now fondly thought of families and I can't emphasise enough how grateful I will always be to 'mi hermana maravillosa Sonya y su familia' We exchanged gifts and promises to keep in touch, before a very emotional series of farewells. I parted from the rest of the group as they went on to New York, while I continued on home, having already planned a trip to the Big Apple six months later with friends. I was sorry to see them go at Newark airport, but the parting was eased somewhat by my having befriended a guy on the plane who invited me into the premier lounge, where we sipped free gin and tonic in relative luxury for four hours courtesy of his platinum pass.

It might seem a somewhat callous attitude following the hardship and poverty we had so recently left behind. But I can honestly say that I appreciate every day how fortunate I am to live in a society a world apart from the degree of deprivation in some of the countries I have visited. I know how some people suffer and I am thankful that I and the people I love don't have to endure such horrors.

The degree of poverty we observed in some areas of Colombia was heart wrenching and I have no idea how people remain so astonishingly positive in the face of such adversity. The accepting nature of the Colombians of their difficulties and their sense of humour in dire situations certainly made for a lot of personal soul searching. They are incredibly religious people and their faith seems hugely instrumental in their constitution, while their pride in their country drives them to hope for and work towards a brighter future for Colombia.

A whole new world

I couldn't write a book about my travels without at least touching upon the mind-blowing underwater world, accessible to anyone who has ever experienced scuba diving. It is difficult to talk about diving in the same way as describing adventures on dry land in different countries, because wherever you go, it is essentially the same experience – just with different colours, different fish and different thickness of wet suit. Plus, there are always people who know far more than you'll ever know, have done more dives than you'll ever do and I'm really no expert.

However, I have been fortunate to dive in a few different places across the world and can honestly say it is one of the most amazing experiences and a lot cheaper than throwing yourself from a plane. Plus, the buzz lasts around sixty minutes instead of sixty seconds and you're less likely to swallow a fly.

I learned to dive in 2002 and spent many weekends off the Cornish and Devon coasts pretty much freezing my bits off and not being able to see much farther than as far as I could reach in front of me. That said, I don't want to be entirely negative about UK diving as there are some great wreck dives and I have friends who frequently dive all over the UK and rave about it. I guess I have resigned myself now to being a warm water diver and that suits me.

A lot of divers will rave about either wrecks or scenic dives, with wreckies balking at those who prefer to look at shoals of pretty fish and scenic divers failing to see the draw of a huge lump of rotting wood. I like both and am just as happy on a beautiful drift dive, floating along with the current, taking in all the diverse life and beautiful colours around me, as I am on an upturned wreckage with nooks and crannies to explore.

It's difficult to be able to say where in the world has the best diving experience and sometimes even if you go to recommended sites, it can still come down to weather conditions, breeding seasons, timing and luck. For example, I have dived from the Poor Knights Islands in the North Island of New Zealand, which is hailed as one of the world's best dive sites and yet my experience was decidedly average. That was until we were back on board, de-rigged and were preparing for the boat to move and someone spotted a hammerhead shark swim around and then under the boat.

I also have a very close friend who has recently completed an open water dive course with the Royal Marines in Phi Phi Island, Thailand – a place I have dived previously and been incredibly underwhelmed by. Yet ironically on his third ever dive, he managed to not only see reef sharks, turtles and moray eels, but had the unique experience of a curious young whale shark checking out their group for several minutes and seemingly playing with the divers who were all close enough to touch its tail.

It is also fair to say that I tend to compare all dive sites to those I did around Bali in 2002 and I accept that because that was my first taste of warm water diving, I may be looking at it through a rose-tinted mask. Bali was everything I had ever imagined warm water diving would be and the colours were breathtaking. I remember my first dive, which was from the shore and we had to precariously teeter down a shingle beach into the water. It didn't matter how deep we went, it was crystal clear and turquoise blue and, as we descended, the fish just surrounded us.

Like any new diver, I was absolutely amazed and couldn't believe how much I could see, the vibrancy of colour and the sheer scale of this new world around me. Once I had settled in to the difference in buoyancy from diving in cold waters and found my comfort zone, the only difficulty I had was not being able to verbalise my excitement and babble on in the irritatingly animated way I do when I get overexcited. We swam deeper and then around a rock outcrop loomed the dark carcass of a wreck. It was a really eerie feeling to see this huge dark shape emerge in front of you and it took me back a little at first, almost as if I expected something menacing from it. I think it just came down to the fact that it seemed to appear out of nowhere and it was so clear.

I have dived on the Great Barrier Reef, which I have to say was a little disappointing due to the unfortunate over-commercialisation of the sites and too many disrespectful divers, who think it won't make any difference if just one person touches the coral or collects a little souvenir.

But probably the best way to dive abroad if you have the time and the inclination is on a 'liveaboard', which is exactly what it says and you spend a few days, a week or longer, literally living aboard a boat. I spent a week doing exactly that in Egypt in 2007 and it was one of the best experiences I have had – both for the diving and the holiday. The diving was unarguably world-class and I was fortunate enough to meet the most fantastic group of friends I have ever made on a holiday and who I am pleased to still be friends with now.

As I have already said though, I won't share every diving experience or talk about the places I still want to dive because it wouldn't be relevant to everyone and would make for quite repetitive reading. All I will say is, I have often taken a few moments to turn away from the reef I am diving and stare out into the endless deep blue of the ocean, where there seems to be no up and no down. At those times, I find myself feeling a little sad that there is no real way to describe to my friends who don't dive, the magical experience of being part of this beautiful, hidden world.

EPILOGUE

In all this time, I don't feel like I've ever had a bad experience – not even being spat at by the angry Vietnamese cyclo driver. Each one is as significant a part of my travels as the next and they make up the colourful memories that I look back on, so often and smile.

I think it is also important to say that despite all of the amazing countries I have visited and the wonderful sights I've been fortunate enough to experience, I still love coming back to the UK. I've always tried to appreciate what is around me and not to take for granted the beautiful countryside and historic cities we have and are envied for, the world over.

I will always remember coming home from Florida after a family holiday in the states in 1996 and realising as we drove home to Kent through the lush green countryside, that I hadn't seen fields, or trees on this scale anywhere we had visited in the US in nearly four weeks.

My parents live in Maidstone, Kent, on the edge of the huge and beautiful Mote Park and I have so many fond memories of walking and playing on the edge of the lake or running through the naturally preserved lawns and conservation areas. The most significant moment for me, in appreciating my surroundings came on my return from New Zealand, when I stayed with my parents for a few days and struggled to sleep from jet lag.

I woke at about 5.30 am one morning in May and it was one of those beautiful, crisp spring mornings, where you know it's going to be a hot day and the sun is just waiting to shine through, once the early morning mist has cleared. I got up and decided to go for a run, taking my usual route through the park and around the lake, past the early fishermen and to the far side, where the willow trees lean over onto the water.

As I ran, I stared out at the lake and the mist seemed to merge into the water, with the reflection of the trees mirrored perfectly on the surface so you almost couldn't tell where tree and sky stopped and their reflection started. I could see my breath in the air, but at the same time feel the warm sun on my skin and I stopped in my tracks. I remember thinking that it was so stunning and so peaceful, that it rivalled any of the scenery I had just left in New Zealand and that I was so amazingly lucky to have this to come home to.

CPSIA information can be obtained
at www.ICGtesting.com
Printed in the USA
2559LVUK00001B